"As a m... how to ... meltdov... clients c...

...you do before the ...ne working with ...ae ...nes!"

—**Christopher Elliott**
Consumer advocate
Ombudsman
National Geographic Traveler

"I've always said the three most important things in business are customer service, customer service, and customer service. Now I'll add a fourth—read this book!"

—**Dayna Steele**
Speaker, business consultant, and author of
Rock to the Top: What I Learned about Success from the World's Greatest Rock Stars

"There is no question that customer service and, even more, customer perception can make or break your business. I am glad that social media über-guru Peter Shankman has finally deigned to share his secrets with the rest of us. This book belongs in every businessperson's library. It's in mine!"

—**Charles Justiz**
Retired NASA pilot and author of *Specific Impulse*

"Peter's a buzzsaw of ideas. The big risk is that your head will explode before you implement this all. The beauty of a book is that you can read it slowly. Peter's mind moves so fast that, were you to receive these ideas in person, you couldn't possibly write fast enough to keep up."

—**Chris Brogan**
President, Human Business Works, and publisher
chrisbrogan.com

"Peter Shankman gets his kicks jumping out of perfectly good airplanes. As it turns out, that avocation may be an apt analogy for the world of social media. It is rising up to meet you—fast—and if you don't pull the 'tweet' chord in time, you are destined to crater. Shankman offers a compelling, engaging, humorous checklist of do's and don'ts for those who are still in a freefall—a bit dazed—wondering what happened to all the tried-and-true rules of advertising, marketing, and PR. Shankman knows the answer, and he can barely contain his enthusiasm in sharing his insights. He is a leading social networking evangelizer—that is why so many blue-chip companies seek him out. And that is why I selected him to be on the NASA Advisory Council Education and Public Outreach Committee. His advice is not rocket science, but it isn't always what you might predict. As skydivers like to say, you'll be fine so long as you don't do anything stupid. Read this book and you will know how to be smart—in 140 characters or less!"

—Miles O'Brien
formerly of CNN

"I'll give you my favorite piece of advice from Peter right here: don't have a goal of making something viral. Make it good, and it will go viral. Peter shares my belief: don't treat your customers well after something has gone wrong. Treat them well at every interaction."

—Franco Bianchi
President & CEO
Haworth, Inc.

Customer

New Rules for a Social Media World

Service

Peter Shankman

800 East 96th Street,
Indianapolis, Indiana 46240 USA

Customer Service
New Rules for a Social Media World

ISBN-13: 978-0-7897-4709-9
ISBN-10: 0-7897-4709-X

Library of Congress Cataloging-in-Publication Data

Shankman, Peter.
  Customer service : new rules for a social media world / Peter Shankman.
    p. cm.
  Includes index.
  ISBN 978-0-7897-4709-9
  1. Customer services. 2. Internet marketing. 3. Social media. 4. Online social networks. I. Title.
  HF5415.5.S5194 2011
  658.8'12—dc22

                    2010046786

Printed in the United States of America

First Printing: December 2010

Trademarks

Warning and Disclaimer

Bulk Sales

Que Publishing offers excellent discounts on this book when ordered in quantity for bulk purchases or special sales. For more information, please contact

> **U.S. Corporate and Government Sales**
> **1-800-382-3419**
> **corpsales@pearsontechgroup.com**

For sales outside of the U.S., please contact

> **International Sales**
> **international@pearson.com**

Associate Publisher
Greg Wiegand

Acquisitions Editor
Rick Kughen

Development Editor
Rick Kughen

Managing Editor
Kristy Hart

Project Editor
Andrew Beaster

Copy Editor
Megan Wade

Indexer
Cheryl Lenser

Proofreader
Sally Yuska

Technical Editor
Simon Salt

Publishing Coordinator
Cindy Teeters

Interior Designer
Anne Jones

Cover Designer
Anne Jones

Compositor
Gloria Schurick

CONTENTS AT A GLANCE

TABLE OF CONTENTS

About the Author

Peter Shankman—*PR Week Magazine* has described Peter as "redefining the art of networking," and *Investor's Business Daily* has called him "crazy, but effective." Peter Shankman is a spectacular example of what happens when you harness the power of Attention Deficit Hyperactivity Disorder (ADHD) and make it work to your advantage. An entrepreneur, author, speaker, and worldwide connector, Peter is recognized worldwide for radically new ways of thinking about social media, PR, marketing, advertising, creativity, and customer service.

Peter is perhaps best known for founding Help A Reporter Out (HARO), which in under a year has become the de-facto standard for thousands of journalists looking for sources on deadline, offering them more than 125,000 sources around the world looking to be quoted in the media. HARO is currently the largest free source repository in the world, sending out over 1,500 queries from worldwide media each week. HARO's tagline, "Everyone Is an Expert at Something," proves over and over again to be true, as thousands of new members join at helpareporter.com each week.

In addition to HARO, Peter is the founder and CEO of The Geek Factory, Inc., a boutique social media and marketing strategy firm located in New York City, with clients worldwide. His blog (www.shankman.com), which he launched as a website in 1995, both comments on and generates news and conversation.

Peter's PR and social media clients have included the Snapple Beverage Group, NASA, The U.S. Department of Defense, Walt Disney World, The Ad Council, American Express, Discovery Networks, New Frontier Media, Napster, Juno, Dream Catcher Destinations Club, Harrah's Hotels, and many others. In addition, he sits on the board of the Scott-e-Vest, the world's first technologically enabled clothing line.

Peter is the author of *Can We Do That?! Outrageous PR Stunts That Work and Why Your Company Needs Them* (Wiley and Sons 2006) and is a frequent keynote speaker and workshop presenter at conferences and tradeshows worldwide, including The Public Relations Society of America, The International Association of Business Communicators, CTIA, CTAM, CES, PMA, OMMA, Mobile Marketing Asia, and the Direct Marketing Association.

A marketing pundit for several national and international news channels, including Fox News, CNN, and MSNBC, Peter is frequently quoted in major media and trade publications, including *The Wall Street Journal*, *Los Angeles Times*, *New York Daily News*, Associated Press, Reuters, CNN, and *USA Today*.

Peter started his career in Vienna, Virginia, with America Online as a senior news editor. He helped found the AOL Newsroom and spearheaded coverage of the Democratic and Republican 1996 conventions, which marked the first time an online news service covered any major political event.

Born and raised in New York City, Peter still lives there with his two psychotic cats, Karma and NASA, who consistently deny his repeated requests to relinquish the couch. In the few hours of spare time Peter has per month, he's a frequent runner, with 13 completed marathons and countless triathlons to his credit, and is a "B" licensed skydiver, specializing in free-flying.

Dedication

For Grandma Betty

Acknowledgments

A few people made this book possible…

Thank you to all of my clients for the inspiration and ideas you've given me along the way.

Massive thanks to everyone in the HARO Family, for helping me grow my baby into a powerhouse that continues to change the very face of journalism and public relations.

Thanks to my editor, Rick Kughen, for helping me get this project out the door despite my massive ADHD.

Mom and Dad, thanks, as always, for the support and unconditional love.

Finally, thanks to my most amazing assistant, Meagan Walker, not only for keeping me on track with this project, but for keeping my life on track, and making sure I stay on target, all the time, without ever becoming annoying.

We Want to Hear from You!

As the reader of this book, *you* are our most important critic and commentator. We value your opinion and want to know what we're doing right, what we could do better, what areas you'd like to see us publish in, and any other words of wisdom you're willing to pass our way.

As an associate publisher for Que Publishing, I welcome your comments. You can email or write me directly to let me know what you did or didn't like about this book—as well as what we can do to make our books better.

Please note that I cannot help you with technical problems related to the topic of this book. We do have a User Services group, however, where I will forward specific technical questions related to the book.

When you write, please be sure to include this book's title and author as well as your name, email address, and phone number. I will carefully review your comments and share them with the author and editors who worked on the book.

Email: feedback@quepublishing.com

Mail: Greg Wiegand
            Associate Publisher
            Que Publishing
            800 East 96th Street
            Indianapolis, IN 46240 USA

Reader Services

Visit our website and register this book at informit.com/register for convenient access to any updates, downloads, or errata that might be available for this book.

When I was a clueless sophomore at Boston University in 1992, I was taking the Amtrak from my home in New York City back to Boston right after winter break. The East Coast was living up to its freezing reputation. About halfway through the trip, the train suddenly lurched to a stop. We sat in the very quiet cars for a bit, unsure of what was going on. Eventually, the conductor got on the PA system and said, "We're having some kind of electrical problem with this train; everybody out."

It was around 8 p.m., it was freezing, and we were some-where between New York and Boston. But we got out and waited—not even at a station, but "near" one—for three hours, in the cold, until another train showed up. When it did, we got on (now having no seats because this train was already full) and stood the next four hours until we arrived in Boston.

It was what it was because we had no other options. We got off the train in Boston, seven hours late, tired, cranky, *and cold. We went home and went to sleep. The next morning, Amtrak continued on and no one in the world was any the wiser that 400 or so people were majorly inconvenienced. It was what it was, and Amtrak knew it. "Oh well," they probably said. "We still got paid."*

Several months ago, I was giving a speech at a hotel in Florida. About 20 minutes before my speech, the Wi-Fi in the hotel went out. I couldn't connect to save my life, and of course, I wanted to show my audience a video from YouTube.

I pulled out my BlackBerry and sent a message (see Figure 1) to Twitter: "Dear Omni Hotel, Jacksonville: Your key lime pie: Win. But your Wi-Fi: FAIL."

Eight minutes later, a technician from Omni Hotels walked into my conference, with t-minus 12 minutes until my speech. He asked, "Is the Wi-Fi down for you, sir? I'm going into the basement and rebooting the router. Stand by, ok?"

Three minutes later, I was online, downloading my video as my audience was starting to walk in and take their seats. I quickly sent another tweet, reading, "Omni Hotels Customer Service: FTW! (For The Win!)"

Omni Hotels saw a problem, responded to it in real time, and made me a fan for life.

Figure 1 *Customer feedback has never been this instant.*

Why? Because Laurie Kopstad, Revenue Manager at the Omni Jacksonville Hotels, plays by the new rules of customer service. She saw an opportunity to turn a complainer into a fan. She took the opportunity, and it paid off. All it took was one walkie-talkie dispatch to the tech asking him to look into and resolve a problem. She turned a small complaint into a huge win for her hotel, while preventing it from becoming a big problem. More importantly, Laurie saw the benefits in *listening*.

Omni Hotels rocks. And I'm not afraid to tell you so. As a matter of fact, I'll go out of my way to make sure you know. Does your company rock the new rules of customer service in the age of social media? For your sake, you better hope so.

If you've bought this book on Amazon, or if you're reading it in a bookstore while sipping a latte, chances are, it's because you run a business or are in charge of the public face of one and you're seeing the changes all around you. You're watching people have great customer service experiences because you're reading about them on Facebook or you're noticing them being "tweeted," even if you're not entirely sure what that means.

You're also seeing companies get in serious trouble when they don't take their customer problems seriously. You've noticed some groundswells, and you've seen some movements. You've even noticed that all of your friends have stopped going to one specific store—or even better, they're all going to one specific store. People started mentioning things such as "United Breaks Guitars," or "Kevin Smith and Southwest" and you realized that something was up.

And you're thinking, "Gee, maybe I should get into that."

Yeah. You probably should.

Let's get some things out of the way first: Who am I, and why are you listening to me?

I've been fortunate enough to have been working in this industry since before it was an industry. I've watched customer service go from "the customer is always right" to "the customer can kill you in under 120 characters." I've seen hundreds of companies rise to the top of their game using the new rules of customer service, and seen thousands of them fall to the ground and be decimated by not believing the rules applied to them.

I've been "online" in one capacity or another since 1983, when I got my first computer and incredibly slow modem. When I got out of college, I started my career as one of the first editors in the America Online newsroom (Keyword: News) down in Vienna, Virginia. AOL had less than a few million people online at that time, and the Web as we know it hadn't been invented yet. "Social media" back then meant you talked about journalism in a bar with some friends.

The thing was, working at AOL gave me an incredible window into customer service. See, I'd spend all day building huge news packages that people could read and download. I'd test them at the office, on a zippy computer with a super-fast Internet connection. Then I'd go home and look at them again with my crappy computer and incredibly slow modem. I'd get truly frustrated because it would take hours to load the same thing that it took seconds to load back in the office.

That's when I realized that—from the largest of companies to the smallest of mom-and-pop bakeries—the majority of us don't understand the customer experience.

We run our companies the way we want to and then wonder why our customers leave when we refuse to change. We don't listen to our customers because we are sure we know better than them. And then we're shocked when they go somewhere else.

When I left AOL and started The Geek Factory, Inc.—my own PR firm in New York—I promised myself that I'd go to any extent to make sure that my clients understood that I understood them. The biggest problem clients of PR agencies had (and continue to have) is that they feel like they're a small fish in a big pond of clients. Agencies take tons of time to return calls, and they take almost as long to respond to emails. In short, they don't give a crap. In some ways, that's why they're agencies. If they cared more, they'd be working for the company in-house.

I vowed my agency would never be that way. And I vowed to do it in one unique way:

Pizza.

(This is the first of many points in this book where you scratch your head and assume I'm just insane.)

Pizza? What does pizza have to do with good customer service?

Well, here's the deal: The majority of agencies bill by the hour. They spend all their time billing and billing, rounding up every 5 minutes so harshly that in the end, you're afraid to call them, lest dialing their number equates to a $100 charge. And if you're afraid to call them, well, they're not going to be much good to you.

In short, PR firms act like law firms.

I simply decided that I was never going to bill hourly, and, once every few months, I was going to show up at a client's office, armed with nothing more than a few pizza pies, right around lunchtime. I wasn't going to bill the client, and I wasn't going to charge them for the pizza. Rather, I'd show up, find my contact, and then simply ask whomever was in the office to join us, have some pizza, and talk.

The first time I did this, the client thought I was insane. The conversation was primarily them asking me why I was doing this. They didn't truly understand that my agency was different. We were bringing them pizza and not charging for it. The best part was that we weren't doing so to curry favor or to prove that we thought differently than other agencies (that was just a nice byproduct). Rather, we were bringing in pizza, on a random Wednesday, for no other reason than this:

We wanted to listen.

We wanted to listen to the client. We wanted them to talk to us. We wanted them to tell us what they were working on. Tell us what they were doing that could potentially lead to new ways of talking about them. What stuff were they doing that we could publicize? What ideas were they thinking about that we could look at from "outside" the box and perhaps put a new spin on?

Once clients realized why we were doing it, they were incredibly appreciative. In fact, we got every single client we ever had through current client referrals. And in an entirely service-based industry such as PR, that's huge. It says something important about what we had built.

We quickly became the agency known as "the pizza agency." But in reality, all we were doing was listening. And in a world where there's too much noise and not enough signal, listening is critical.

I once dated a woman from the South whose mother had all these very funny "Southern sayings." I don't remember most of them (the majority of them involved food and usually ended in "Shug"), but the one I do remember was this: "God gave you two ears and one mouth so you could listen twice as much as you talk, Shug."

The daughter and I broke up, but I'll never forget her mom's comment—so accurate, even with the Southern drawl.

I'd always been a listener. Malcolm Gladwell calls people like me "connectors." We know lots of people, and we put them together whenever we see a benefit to them.

I don't know how much of a connector I am, but I do know that I'm blessed with having ADHD—so much so that I rarely sit still. The person I pity the most is the one on the plane seated next to me. Why? Because by the time we land, until he fakes his own death midway through the flight, I'm going to know a lot about him. It's just who I am—and it's paid off in both my personal and professional lives.

As I started flying more and more for work, and meeting more and more people, I started collecting quite the Rolodex of the most random people in the world—a child psychologist who only treats high-risk youth. The head of music education for the city of New York. A former Navy SEAL. Skydivers. You name it.

As I listened to their stories and thought, "Wow, they have a great story—I should remember this person!" And over time, I was remembering more and more people.

Then one day, I had an epiphany: What if I let all my journalist friends know about all the people I knew? Not to benefit my clients or anything, but just to be helpful?

So on a cold winter day in 2004, I sent my first "Good Karma Email" to about 150 journalists. It went something like this:

Dear Jonathan,

Consider this a PR guy's attempt at good karma for a Sunday afternoon, when it's snowing, and quite frankly, just too cold to go outside into the freezing depths of Manhattan. So I'm sitting on my couch with my two psychotic cats (http://www.geekfactory.com/geekcats.htm) and figured it was a good time to do my yearly "PR karma."

First off, this is SO not a pitch. Quite the opposite. This is an offer of help. I do this about once a year—the media seem to like it.

In a nutshell, I'm inviting you to source me. Add me to your email list when you're desperately seeking a quote at 11 minutes to deadline. Call me when something major breaks. Put me in your Rolodex, and feel free to dial.

And, no, this is not to get me in the press.

Basically, I just know a LOT of people. Between the amount of time I travel for business (in excess of 200k miles a year), the number of advisory boards on which I sit, the amount of clients I have, and the fact that I'm just a talkative (some might say hyperactive), nice, ADHD guy who only sleeps about four hours a night to begin with, I have a Palm Pilot bursting at the seams.

This isn't about my clients, by the way. In fact, they're the smallest category. Mostly it's people I've become friends/colleagues with in some capacity, who do the most random things. Identity theft investigators. Litigators who only work on animal-related lawsuits. The guy who manufactures the laces that are used in 75 percent of the world's sneakers. Knitters who only knit with soy, bamboo, or hemp yarn. The Director of Arts Education for the NYC Department of Education. A director of security for a large nationwide upscale department store. A child psychologist who only works with high-risk, suicidal kids. A guy with over 5,000 skydives under his belt. A former Navy SEAL who now teaches mortals like me how to stay in shape. A guy who designs solar clothing that lights up with messages on the back. All friends, people I've met on airplanes (or while jumping out of them), at sushi dinners, while running marathons, or while swimming the Escape From Alcatraz Triathlon (which was, as expected, REALLY cold).

Really RANDOM people—I happen to know them. Mostly because I do really random things.

I also have some great clients—Dream Catcher Retreats, AirTroductions, OpSec Security, and a bunch of others. In addition, I throw a good number of events and parties during the year and am constantly looking for members of the media who would enjoy attending. If that's you, let me know as well. See, I don't sleep much.

So, like I said, consider it good karma. I run a PR shop in New York called The Geek Factory, Inc. (www.geekfactory.com). If I'm able to offer you a source that winds up helping you get in under a deadline or makes a story more colorful, then cool. If it helps a client, great, but if it doesn't, like I said, it's all about karma. Who knows where it will lead?

Anyhow, source me. That's my offer for this afternoon. My contact information is below. Add me to whatever Rolodex you're currently using, and if I can help in any way, feel free to call.

All the best,

Peter Shankman

CEO

The Geek Factory, Inc.

P.S. Don't worry—this isn't a list from which you need to be removed. I won't start sending out weekly updates or anything, I promise. And to answer the second most frequently asked question, I got your name from Media Map, the PR/journalist tool.

I got back about 10 or so emails immediately, all of which said, "Why are you contacting me? You must want something. Don't email me again." Or something concise like that. And that's fine. You're always going to encounter fear-based resistance when you create something new.

But then, I got an email from a reporter at a small newspaper on the West Coast who said something to the extent of, "I don't know if this is real or a joke, but what the heck, I'm desperate. Do you know anyone who knows about the new Dell laptops that are coming out next week?"

One phone call later, I'd connected this reporter with someone who'd used Dell computers exclusively and was a member of several Dell chat rooms. The reporter sent me an email after the story ran, saying, "Hey, thanks Peter. Not sure what you get out of it, but I appreciate the help!"

What the reporter didn't know then was how much I really was getting out of it! I was starting to become known as "that guy"—you know, the guy who everyone emails or calls when they have a question or a problem. The guy who knows everyone.

RULE: You want to be "that guy."

That guy has an incredible amount of power. That guy knows what's going on, has his ear to the ground at all times, and gets the most valuable information given to him when it happens. He's the guy who avoids the line at the restaurant or bar, who's escorted past the velvet rope.

Why? Because "that guy" knows everyone and is valuable to everyone.

Why? Because that guy listens.

That one "good karma" email I sent back in 2004 has now turned into a 3x per day, 100,000 member mailing list, with close to 1,500 reporter queries sent each week. It's turned into a full-fledged company called Help A Reporter Out (HARO: www. helpareporter.com). It's free and is supported by a small little text ad at the top of each email. Those ads currently sell for $1,500 a piece, and we're normally sold out four months in advance.

All this because I listen to people.

It's all about customer service. We never spent a penny on advertising. Rather, we've let word-of-mouth do the trick. I respond personally to every email I receive, usually within a few minutes. (Try it—peter@shankman.com). I talk to people personally. My assistant is in charge of my schedule, not because I don't want to do it, but because I'm so scattered across the globe that I'll screw it up. But never has a person told me that he couldn't get in touch with me. It simply doesn't happen. I listen, I respond, and I help when I can.

That's customer service.

It doesn't matter whether your company is one person, or a million people. People want to know they matter. They want to know they're listened to. And the best (and only) way to do that is to actually do it. I try and do that every single day.

That's customer service.

I respond when people tweet me, and I comment when they post on my Facebook wall. I forward their resumes if I know them and know they're looking for a job. I can be reached.

That's customer service.

More important than ever, my customer service is mixed with speed. In today's economy, speed is life. People post on Facebook, tweet on Twitter, and blog on their blogs because it's instantaneous. Have a bad experience at a restaurant? You're in the moment. You want the world to be in the moment with you.

For the first time in history, we have the ability to do that, and it's only going to get more intense.

It's no longer about "Oh, I wish I had a camera." In the next few years, you won't be able to buy a mobile phone *without* a camera! What does that mean? It means 365 million citizen journalists walking this country alone, each one ready to broadcast photos of your screw-up within 5 seconds of it happening.

You think photos are bad? What about video? Mobile video is just starting to come of age. Today, I was in line at security at Newark Airport. They had two of seven lanes open, and about 10 TSA agents were standing around talking and not working. I took out my BlackBerry, took 12 seconds of video of the agents standing around, and uploaded it to 12seconds.tv. In 30 seconds 61,000 people who follow me on Twitter @petershankman) knew that the TSA agents at Newark Airport were caught on film not doing their jobs.

What if it wasn't a government agency with no need to get better? What if it was your restaurant? Or your company? Or your store? It's happening more and more, every single day.

There are no guaranteed ways to make sure this doesn't happen to you because at some point, it's going to. What you can make sure of is that it happens so infrequently that it's just a blip on the radar screen. More importantly, you can be so well versed on the new rules of customer service that when it *does* happen, not only do you take the steps to correct it, but you have an army of fans, made up of happy customers, who will immediately come to your defense. And when you've achieved that, you've built a wonderful customer service landing pillow for yourself to cushion the inevitable bumps and bruises you'll encounter along the way.

That's what we're going to do here. Through practical, real-life examples of both social media customer service wins and losses, we're going to build you that pillow. The goal of this book is to arm you with the tools to grow your business, using your number-one resource—your customers—and also to provide the emergency beacons to help guide you back when the occasional disaster strikes.

If I wanted you to take away one rule from this book, it's this:

For 99.9% of us, we don't listen anywhere near enough. And not listening is the leading cause of failure in today's economy. Not listening to our customers, not listening to our advisors, not listening to the markets, not listening to the wind. We need to become a society that again learns the power of listening.

If you're willing to let me, I'd like to help you learn once again how to listen.

Bruce Hornsby once wrote, "That's just the way it is. Some things will never change." Except when they do. Keep reading. Let's change some things.

Putting Together a Social Media Team

"All battles are won long before they're ever fought."
Sun Tzu

I love watching companies create social media "teams." They pull together some of the smartest people from marketing, some of the smartest people from PR, and a high-level executive to run the whole thing. Then they sit and plan for what they're going to say for each and every possible thing a customer could potentially write, tweet, or post online. I've seen charts of this stuff that are 50–75 pages long.

One problem, though...

None of the people on the social media team *have ever spent any time talking to a customer.*

Can you imagine the President's Cabinet made up of no one with any political experience? Yet for some reason, almost all companies think that way—and then they're shocked (shocked!) to find that they're not communicating with their customers in the best way possible.

Fact is, you use the right people for the right jobs. I'm not saying don't put a PR person and a high-level exec on the team, but make damn sure that the team includes not only a few customer service people, but even more importantly, customer service people the rest of the team will listen to!

At the end of the day, the team is only as good as the advice it receives. If no one knows how to interact with the customer, the customer service portion of your social media plan is gonna, well, the scientific term is *suck*.

Let's try to avoid sucking, ok?

This chapter introduces you to how I suggest you structure your social media team. Then, I show you what your audience is likely to look like. This chapter is designed to give you a taste of what you'll see once you build your social media team. We'll talk about how the teams should behave and what tools they should use later in the book.

Meet Your Team

Putting together your social media team is something that you should do carefully and only after some planning. In this section, I show you how I believe a social media team should be set up.

YOUR MILEAGE MAY VARY

Your primary social team might vary, depending on how big your company is, how many people want to get involved, and so on. In general, however, the people I describe in this section will be your "go-to" group—the one that's going to work with you and create and implement your social media plan for your company. Get to know them well.

One thing to remember is that, chances are, you have several social media gurus (one might know Facebook, one might know blogging, and so on) in your company already. They're probably just too scared to come out and let you know. So be loud. You're building a social media team, and you want the world to know about it! Remember high school, when you'd put up 100 signs all over school letting people know about the French Club meeting after school? Same thing here. Got a company newsletter? You want people to know what you're doing, not only because it fosters intracompany communication, but also because it'll bring out some of the best and brightest of your company who you likely didn't even know worked there.

The Customer Service People

No one realizes it, but the customer service people simply have to be the heart of your social media team. If your social media plan involves listening and reacting to the customer (and it better!), then not having customer service people on your social media team is a waste of both your team's goals and your customer service goals as a whole.

The customer service team is more than likely the most integral part of your company. They're the first line of attack *and* defense when it comes to customer communication. They know more about the customer in one day than most of your company knows in a month. Does one of your products have a specific problem? They know before anyone. Is a node down in Portsmouth, New Hampshire? They know before your IT people do. Did an agent bump a customer off a plane in Casper, Wyoming without cause? They're going to hear about it first. Even more importantly, they're going to know the right way to react. Remember—it's all they do.

By putting one or more customer service people on your social media team, you're ensuring social media will do what it's intended to do: help you communicate better with your audience. Remember this: Tech people are tech people for a reason. They love to communicate with inanimate objects. The same goes for marketers. They love to communicate with ads, rate cards, and job bags. Ad guys? They love to communicate with logos.

Customer service people communicate with the customers. Make sure they're part of your social media team. Being able to communicate with your customers should always, always, always be the first rule of your social media strategy.

The PR Person

The PR person almost always gets asked to be a part of the social media team. I don't know exactly how PR got thrown into the mix in the first place. It's probably because the first people to play with social media were PR people who thought of it as a new way to reach journalists.

 Note

By the way, reaching out blindly to journalists via social media can have disastrous results. Don't do this until you read this entire book. Sending a Facebook message to a reporter out of the blue will more than likely result in your untimely death. Trust me.

The PR person is actually a useful mammal to have on the team since the PR person is the one who actually helps craft the company message. They make sure the company stays on point and isn't giving two or three different messages each time they say something. Imagine if you have five people listening and responding on Twitter. This can result in two different people getting two different answers to the same question. Yikes! So listen to the PR person, no doubt. Another nice bonus is that the PR people usually get the best invites to corporate events and parties, so it's good to be their friend.

The High-Level Exec

Ah, the high-level exec. This person is always a bit hard to get a read on. On one hand, she knows that a good social media plan can catapult you into the stratosphere. If you're lucky, this person understands the benefits of a social media plan, trusts you enough to let you run it, and generally will run interference between you and the higher-ups who constantly use the phrase "that team with their Twitter and stuff." If that's the case, you're good to go. Let the exec help you clear the oodles of red tape by keeping her in the loop. Use a system I came up with years ago called ROAR (Responsibility, Opportunity, Awareness, Results):

- **Responsibility**—You've proven that you can take charge of the situation and, without question, produce a stellar social media plan for your entire organization.

- **Opportunity**—You've done your homework and can show why a good social media plan is critical to your company's success.

- **Awareness**—You've shown that you're familiar with the potential pitfalls of social media; you're making sure that your company's roadmap has ways around them; and you have multiple backup plans not only for a potential crisis, but for success, as well.

- **Results**—Finally, after all is said and done, you need to be able to show your high-level exec what you've done, both from a 10-foot view and a 50,000-foot view, so she can run it up the flagpole, giving you clearance for your next big idea.

By following the ROAR system, you're guaranteeing that you'll keep your high-level exec on your side—something you're going to desperately need when you're trying to convince the bean counters why they should send you to the hottest social media show or let you purchase that new Flip Mino HD Camera.

The Marketing Guys

The marketing guys aren't the same guys as the PR guys. Marketing thinks of PR as an afterthought and primarily focuses on advertising—getting the "brand message" out there and, to a degree, advertising, logos, and so on. Work with these guys to make sure the social media team is on point in terms of how the logo of the company looks, that the social media backgrounds are similar to that of the company logo (but with a little more flair), and that key messaging statements are the same.

Another good thing about marketing is that they usually have access to the best SWAG (stuff we all get). These t-shirts, hats, free memberships to things, and so on are great prizes when you're offering giveaways on your site and the like.

The Guy from Accounting Who Has a Facebook Page

This guy is the most dangerous of them all but can also be a kind ally. He might not be from accounting. He might be from management, or work in the shipping department, or—even worse—be the son of the boss.

Whoever he is, you have to accept that people hear the word *Facebook, Twitter,* or even simply *Web* and assume that, well, "Hey, they have a Twitter account! They can help!"

Yes and no. The fact is that employees who aren't specifically a part of your social media plan can be a tremendous ally, but they also can sink your project faster than the Titanic. If they happen to know a lot, by all means, recruit them into your team. You'll be a kind, benevolent boss who brings in someone who knows something the others don't. This person can be helpful, if you allow it. This person can also wind up being an evangelist for your company in ways you've never thought of. But again, this is only going to happen if he's good, and only if he's willing to work with the team.

On the flipside, you want to make sure—if he truly can't be ignored—that you give him busy-work to not get in your way. If this person feels involved, you can utilize his skills and get rid of some of the annoying busy-work that hits every once in a while. For example, you could ask him to research various Facebook groups and so on—stuff that needs to be done but might keep slipping off your radar.

Keep in mind, however, that when these "walk-ins" come in, you should treat them with an open mind and listen to them. Some of your most loyal company evangelists might be the kid with the blog who never thought he could help—until he shows up with Wordpress theme after Wordpress theme. All of a sudden, he's one of your most valuable assets. Remember these people.

The Flip Side: Meet Your Audience

Now that you know what your social media team should look like, you need to know what your audience is likely to look like. As we know, this is just a rough guideline. You're going to meet many more people in your day-to-day world navigating the social media landscape. But this should be a good start. If nothing else, it gives you something to look for.

The One-time Complainer

Chances are, the people you're going to meet most often are those who have somehow been "wronged" by your company, an employee, or a product. This will usually occur via one of two three ways:—via Facebook, a blog, or Twitter. If you're smart and have your Google Alerts set up, you'll be notified if the complainer pops up anywhere else first. (We'll get to those later in the book.)

You'll want to make sure you notice the-one-time-complainer immediately, using the tools at your disposal. If you're smart, a customer service person on your social media team will notice and can engage the complainer almost instantly, fixing whatever problem exists immediately, and hopefully on the first try. @comcastcares (http://twitter.com/comcastcares) is a Twitter account set up by Comcast Cable. When someone tweets about her cable being out or some other cable issue, Comcast can immediately reach out through Twitter, usually cutting through hours of customer service calls and red tape.

The one-time-complainer can actually be very helpful. If you can fix her problem immediately, you not only turn an angry customer into a happy customer, but you can also notice any trends that might be brewing. Say, perhaps a section of your market has suddenly lost power or a timing circuit blew in one of your games. Having one of your customer service people monitoring the chatter, as it were, can be tremendously beneficial for you.

The Constant Complainer

Strangely, the constant complainer isn't that big of a threat to you. Think about that cousin we all have, the one who is always complaining about something. His job sucks. He can't find a girlfriend. He hates his apartment. What happens after a while? You stop listening to him. You brush off his complaints with a roll of your eyes—after all, you've heard it all before and you don't take him seriously anymore. The same thing happens with the constant complainers. In the end, no one takes them seriously. Of course, you should try to solve his problem. But remember that the constant complainer isn't as important as the one-time-complainer because most likely, no one listens to the constant complainer that closely anymore, anyway.

The Axe-to-Grind

So what creates an axe grinder? Perhaps something happened with this person that went beyond the simple "I'm not pleased." Perhaps she feels that your initial response wasn't "big" enough. Maybe she happens to be an attorney. Whatever the case, the axe-to-grind complainer can cause you a world of hurt. If these complainers have the time, the inclination, and the computer, they can start Facebook groups, buy domain names, call the local media, whatever they feel like. The axe-to-grind complainer should be dealt with the same as you would the one-time complainer.

The Happy Customer

Every once in a while, your social media team will smile, for they've noticed something like this: "Had a problem with my car, called dealership, they fixed it in 20 minutes! Harry's Honda ROCKS!" Yes, we love those. You can use these people. Engage them in conversation. Offer them a coupon or a thank-you discount. Ask if you can use them as a testimonial. Turn a fan into a raving fan. And enjoy it.

The Prima Donna

A prima donna is a customer who feels that he has a big enough following in social media to use it to bully your nascent social media team into giving him what he wants, which is usually disproportionate to the actual or even perceived "hurt" your company caused him.

This is where your mixed discipline team really comes into its own. PR folks are used to handling journalists who act like divas. Customer service people are experienced with the "I want to talk to your manager now" types. With these skill sets combined, your team becomes more than a match for this type of audience member.

End result

I always think of dealing with groups, whether customers, clients, or employees, as taking a morning subway commute. You're going to get the nice smiling guy, then the idiot on her iPhone who won't get out of your way. You'll have the person who is always willing to let you look at his newspaper, then the moron who's eating a really, really smelly sandwich.

Your job is to remain calm and most of all, fluid—know that you're going to encounter these people all the time. Find a way to not only deal with them, but to extract the best out of all of them—no matter how bad or great they are. You never know, the multi-complainer (or iPhone girl) might become your best ally when you least expect it.

At the end of the day, though, without customers, clients, and employees, you've got nothing. If you're truly passionate about increasing the awesomeness of your customer service, your job is to identify, understand, and work with each type of customer, client, and employee—the best way possible.

That makes for an awesomely solid foundation.

Examples of When It Doesn't Work (and What Happens)

You never want to hear the words "uh oh." It's so rare that anything good ever comes immediately after "uh oh." You never hear "Uh oh, I just won the lottery," or "Uh oh, that supermodel said she wants to date me."

No, "uh oh" is usually followed by "the server just went down," or "we just lost our #2 engine," or "did I forget to pack my parachute?"

Yeah, the general consensus? "Uh oh" sucks.

So it was with a lot less than happiness when I uttered the term "uh oh" in February of 2009. I was holding a conference call for about 700 or so people, all of whom had paid $50 per head to attend. The conference call was about how best to pitch the media and included reporters *from the* Wall Street Journal, *the* New York Times, *and the* Los Angeles Times, *to name a few.*

I'd been promoting the call for a few months in advance. It was definitely a "Peter Shankman produced" call, and everyone knew it. It was a big one, too. We'd gotten a bit of media coverage about it because everyone always wants to know how to best get their stories into the press.

Well, 2 p.m. EST came and the call started. I'd received an instant message saying that we'd surpassed 700 people, the largest number we'd ever had on one of these calls. And those were just 700 people who'd paid for the call—who knew how many were listening in conference rooms, around tables, in offices, etc.? This was huge, and I was psyched. I made brief introductions of each reporter and asked them to talk a bit about themselves. Then, about 5 minutes into the call, I started with my prepared questions. As we got to question number three, probably about 10 minutes into the hour-long call, I heard a slight, 1-second "hiccup" on the call quality. I guess that's the best way to describe it. Just a small "blip," like we lost the signal for a second.

No big deal, the call kept going. But then, another blip. And then another. And then, within 20 seconds, we no longer heard the call. Instead, we heard nothing but beeps and blips. We'd lost the call.

I was shell-shocked. I vaguely remember saying something like "Obviously, the call can't continue with the quality listed, so we'll regroup and we'll make the call happen again as soon as we figure out what happened."

Then I went out onto my office's balcony and wished like hell that I hadn't quit smoking several years ago because right then, I wanted a cigarette more than I ever had in my life.

I walked back inside and forced myself to sit down. I applied my crisis rules—listen, understand, plan, and respond (LUPR, or *looper*, as I call them):

- **Listen** to your audience and figure out exactly why they're mad. What specifically pissed them off? What got them so angry? Who was responsible for it?

- **Understand** what happened. Understand why it happened and what caused it to happen. Don't waste a ton of time on this right away, but make sure you have the key facts down.

- **Plan** to fix the problem. Always go in with a plan. Even if it's a quick, three-point plan, have one. Refer to it. Write it in pencil, so you can adapt and change it as needed. But have one!

- **Respond** to your audience. Some say this should be the first step—and they have a point, sort of. You need to respond or react as quickly as possible. However, before you can get in front of the problem, you have to have a plan that you've created by understanding what went wrong and listening to why your audience is angry. Without LUP, R is useless.

Now then—full disclosure—the LAST thing you feel like you want to do in a social media–fueled world is apply a strategy like LUPR when something blows up. Rather, you want to tweet, Facebook, text, carrier pigeon the words "OMG I'M SO SORRY!" and leave it at that. You also want to fight back against everyone who's saying bad things about you. That's totally understandable. It's human nature.

The problem is that rarely works. If you do that, it's almost guaranteed that your words, written during a massive moment of frustration, will come back to bite you. No doubt.

RULE: Don't post in moments of anger, frustration, or sadness.

Okay. So you've taken a deep breath and realized that you're going to have to do a few things first before you start talking to the world.

For me, I had to understand what happened. I needed to understand it from a technical perspective, and I had to put myself in my customers' heads—all 700 or so of them who just paid $50 for 10 minutes of information and 50 minutes of static.

So for me, the *U* (understand) in LUPR was quick and easy. We promised something to our audience. They paid for it based on that promise. We couldn't deliver it, and we now had to make good.

As for the *L* (listen) in LUPR, a quick scan of Twitter told me the story. Some of the comments I read included

"Can anyone else get sound from the call?" "Call quality sucks!"
"What happened?" "@petershankman, WTF? We paid $50 for this?"

They were pissed off, and rightly so. They were confused, and rightly so. They felt cheated, and rightly so. Okay. Got it.

As for the *P* (plan) in LUPR, that was simple: GET ANOTHER CALL GOING AS SOON AS POSSIBLE. To do that, I called all the reporters on the original failed call, silently praying that they could all make the call at the same time the following day. The fates smiled on me. Next, I called the conference call company and told them I'd yell at them later, but right now, they had to make the call work, exactly 23 hours from now. I may have thrown in a comment about how my audience of 50,000 people on Twitter and 20,000 people on Facebook would know that I blamed them if this wasn't fixed.

Whether that was true or not (it wasn't), I had to say it. The call had to happen, and it had to be *flawless*.

After we planned and created a remedy, the next step had to be taken. And it was the hardest: The *R* (respond) in LUPR.

Here are some helpful hints about responding:

- Take five deep, cleansing breaths before you type anything.

- Make sure your laptop is NOT connected to the Internet until you've finished your response, walked away, come back, looked at it again, shown it to a trusted friend (and an attorney, if necessary), and are truly ready to send it. There's nothing worse than putting a mistake out there on top of a mistake.

- Remember what Ice-T said in *New Jack City*: "This is business. It's never personal." Don't let emotions dictate what you write, no matter how much you may want to. (Or maybe that was Wesley Snipes. I don't remember. But the point is still true.)

My response had to be clear-cut, be definite, and get the message across as quickly and firmly as possible: "I screwed up, and I'm gonna fix it."

This is what I posted on my blog within an hour of the call going to Hell:

RESPONSE FROM PETER SHANKMAN AND HARO REGARDING
TODAY'S CONFERENCE CALL
First things first:
Today's HARO "How to Pitch Business Reporters" will be rescheduled for
tomorrow, Thursday, February 19th, at 2pm (14:00) EST.
Now then:
To my esteemed panelists, and to all the audience members listening in: I'm
truly sorry. While the problem was caused by technical issues, the fact is, I
organized the call, I promoted it, my panel convened at my request, and the
audience paid for it on my recommendation. As such, I accept full responsibility
for today's SNAFU, regardless of what caused it.
We don't know exactly what happened. What I do know is that I've used
Conference Call University for our previous two calls, without any problems at
all. We've never had so much as a blip of trouble on either of the previous calls,
and had no reason to expect any different. Obviously, that's not what
happened today.
I truly apologize to each and every one of you, and I vow to make this right.
Tomorrow's conference call will take place at 2pm EST, just like today's did.
CCU will be responsible for giving out the conference call dial-in number for the
audience members. For the panel members, I will call each of you personally an
hour before the call and give you the dial-in numbers.
One final time: I'm truly sorry. For those who can't make the call tomorrow,
I will personally send you an MP3 of the call the second it finishes saving.
Thank you all for your understanding. If I can answer any further questions,
you know I'm available to you via email – peter@shankman.com, via Twitter
@petershankman, or via a cup of coffee if we're in the same city.
-Peter Shankman
15:00, 02/18/09

And that was it. To the point, simple, and quick. I apologized and I explained what
happened. But *most importantly*, I explained to my audience exactly how I was
going to fix it and what would happen if my "fix" didn't work for any specific audience member.

I knew I had to work fast because the tweets were already going out about how
people wanted refunds, were pissed off, and so on. So the post went up, I tweeted it
out, I cracked another Diet Pepsi, and I waited to see what would happen.

**RULE: There comes a point where you're doing *too* much. Doing too much is just as
bad as doing nothing at all.**

It's important to apologize and get the message out. But then there comes a point
where you've done what you can do and now you have to wait. And that's not a bad
thing. Don't go overboard.

Within 10 minutes, the first comments started appearing, and I was floored—they were positive!

Kary Delaria wrote:
February 18th, 2009 at 3:35 pm
Thank you, Peter. This is a stellar example of how to react when everything hits the fan, even when it was clearly beyond your control. I continue to have the utmost respect for you and am looking forward to trying the call again tomorrow!
Best,
Kary

Amy wrote:
February 18th, 2009 at 3:54 pm
Really impressed with both of you (Peter and Conference Call University) – perfect handling of this situation. Don't beat yourselves up. :0)

Sue Jacques *wrote:*
February 18th, 2009 at 5:11 pm
Peter/Marty,
Thank you for handling this unfortunate event with dignity and grace. You took ownership and accountability and showed all of us all how to handle such circumstances with absolute professionalism. Well done! See you tomorrow...
Respectfully,
Sue Jacques

Chris *wrote:*
February 18th, 2009 at 5:45 pm
Memo to organizations, companies, and decent people everywhere: when something goes wrong, there's an unexpected glitch, or any kind of crisis, do yourself a favor and follow Peter Shankman's fine example. THIS is how to do it right, and it's what keeps us HARO addicts loyal forever.
Kudos all around.

Whew! I mean, really. Talk about feeling better! The best part? By the time the call happened (flawlessly) the next day, we'd actually gained 16 people who wanted to be on the call but couldn't make it the first day!

Hope for the Best, Plan for the Worst

So...what'd we learn?

- While you shouldn't count on things going wrong (psychologically that's bad,) you should always remember that things can. When they do, have the plan ready.

 Note

Always have a plan for what happens if you *succeed* beyond your wildest expectations, too!

- Get the plan into play, but make sure you don't waste too much time making it perfect. Remember the adage *a good plan today is better than a perfect plan tomorrow.*

- Be sure you have a nice bank of goodwill from which you can make a withdrawal. You've played nice in the karmic sandbox, you have tons of customers who will support you, and you're working to get the word out (using these customers, too) that you're going to make this right.

- Remember to breathe.

- Don't respond to negative criticism right away, and don't do it in a public forum until you've calmed down.

- The sun will also come up tomorrow. Never forget that. It might seem dark, but the social media world has a very short memory of bad things. Someone else will make a mistake in a few hours, and you'll fade off the radar screen.

Almost all social media failures have several key components in common:

- Something outside of your control happens—a phone line goes down, a site crashes from too much exposure, and so on.

- You under/over/didn't estimate your audience.

- You didn't think of all the possibilities of what could happen.

More often than not, it's not the thing that's beyond your control. It's usually a simple case of not thinking through all the situations that could have happened.

There was a TV show once that analyzed disasters. It would say, "Disasters don't happen—they're a series of specific micro-events, leading to the disaster itself."

TV, as is it usually is, was dead right. So, let's talk about how to avoid a disaster.

Always Be Aware—It's the Thing You Don't Think of that Can Kill You

No matter how busy you think you are running your business, you need to keep one ear to the ground looking for problems. Remember, problems tend to be immediate surprises, which you had no way of expecting. However, problems also can be things that, when you analyze later, you can see where the cracks started to appear. In fact, you often can plot from point A to point "Problem" and see exactly where the situation went awry.

Keeping your ear to the ground starts within your own organization. It could be as simple as tracking trends as they become trends and implementing solutions before they become huge problems.

When the pain reliever Motrin launched a commercial back in 2008 about how mothers should use Motrin to relieve sore muscles from carrying babies in baby slings, moms everywhere went ballistic. "How insulting," they shouted—not only from the rooftops, but from Twitter, Facebook, and blogs galore. By the time the *New York Times* called me—about eight hours after the story broke—to ask my opinion on the issue, the executives at Motrin, well, probably needed a few Excedrin.

The biggest problem for Motrin wasn't the ad itself. We all have brain farts from time to time, where we, for whatever reason, come up with a bad idea. The problem on Motrin's side, however, was that they didn't respond until about 14 hours later. By this time, the Internet had ample opportunity to not only rake Motrin over the coals, but also to rake them over brand-new coals for not being responsive when they started getting raked over the original coals!

In other words, they weren't listening to the wind, nor did Motrin have one ear to the ground.

Had the makers of Motrin been paying attention to what was happening online, a good portion of their mess could have been avoided with a simple "yeah, that was a stupid commercial; we don't know what we were thinking" blog post a few hours in. Instead, it made international news—and not in a good way.

Now, let's look at the flip side of the coin. Domino's Pizza currently has a TV ad campaign in which they ask people to send in photos of their pizzas. Tons of people sent their photos, but the photo Domino's chose to highlight in its commercial shows the top of the pizza sticking to the box, thus ruining the pizza. What? They chose to use a photo showing the world that they were doing something wrong?! Yup. And it makes perfect sense. It lets Domino's show the world that they know there's a problem and *they're working on fixing it.*

No matter how big the problem, while you might not be able to solve it, you can make it *a lot* less hellish if you simply let people know that you're working on the problem.

What's interesting about the Domino's campaign is that it came fast on the heels of another social media situation involving Domino's, but this one wasn't so fun. A year or so ago, a few Domino's employees posted a rather scary video of themselves, shall we say, not taking the best care in the making of your pizza. They were video-taped shoving cheese up their noses before putting it on the pizza, sneezing directly on the food, and doing several other more-than-gross things (see Figure 2.1).

Figure 2.1   *This is the very definition of a social media nightmare.*

Ew.

Domino's immediately responded by firing the employees and working with the local authorities to have them arrested and prosecuted.

What makes this so interesting is that most companies would use this as an excuse to shy away from social media, thinking "See? It can hurt us!" Domino's, on the other hand, weathered the storm and learned about the power of pictures, video, and social media. Their new advertising campaign was born from social media and, by all accounts, has been incredibly successful.

Understand: You *will* fail at social media at some point. How you choose to react to that failure, and how much you learn from it, determines how well you'll do the next time.

Trust Your Instincts

We have instincts for countless reasons. Millions of years ago, instincts saved us from starving, as well as from walking up to a saber-toothed tiger and trying to pet it. Instincts were designed to help us. They're what has kept the species alive.

However, at some point during our evolution, we decided that we were smarter than our instincts. We decided, "Hey, we're smart people. We have opposable thumbs. (Take that, dogs!) We don't have to listen to our instincts if we don't want to!"

So we didn't. And the Darwin Awards were born. (The Darwin Awards are the Internet's unofficial awards for pure stupidity. These awards are given, posthumously, to people who've died doing amazingly stupid things, thus thinning the herd. Things that often begin with the soon-to-be-award-winner saying, "Hey, hold my beer and watch this!")

From a corporate standpoint, though, instincts are a good thing and should be ignored very, very rarely, if at all. In fact, the only times I can remember where I've gotten into serious professional trouble can all be traced back to one moment where I didn't listen to my instincts.

So, I'm going to urge you to take something away from this book that you'll do every time you're faced with a public decision. For the purposes of sanity, a public decision here can be described as pulling the trigger on a social media campaign of any type, devised by you or anyone you work with or any of your clients.

Before you agree to it/launch it/go public with it, ask yourself this one question:

"Do I feel good about this campaign?"

Then listen to your answer.

Your instincts will tell you the right answer.

Now understand—there's a big difference between instincts and fear. We have both for a reason, and they're both designed to keep us alive. But fear can be overcome. Fear is what I get every time I'm about to jump out of that plane on a skydive. I overcome it because I trust my training and my gear. In fact, fear is what keeps me alive and tells me to do certain things during my skydive that are designed to save my life. The day I'm not slightly afraid of my skydive is the day I've lost respect for the sport and the day the sport will kill me.

Instincts are different, though. Instincts shouldn't be overcome. Instincts should be listened to.

If your gut is telling you that there's something wrong, that something shouldn't be happening, or that you should postpone/cancel/re-create/stand up to the client, then you're probably feeling that for a reason. Your instincts are telling you that, in a manner of speaking, to save your life.

Just promise me that you'll listen to your gut before you go live with a campaign, okay?

That advice in itself might be worth the cost of this book a thousand times over one day, and if it is, I'm glad I could help.

(If it really is, email me at peter@shankman.com and tell me what happened; perhaps I'll use it in an upcoming case study.)

Cooler Heads Prevail

One very important lesson to take away from this book is that you should never argue with your audience. Sadly, Nestle didn't know this.

Nestle posted a rather benign statement on its Facebook page asking people to not use altered versions of its logo as their profile photos. If people used the altered logos, Nestle said, those logos would be removed.

Of course, people started posting that Nestle wasn't allowed to tell them what to do—"you're not the boss of me, blah, blah." Nothing new there.

What happened next, though, was kind of amazing. The person running Nestle's Facebook page decided to start getting into arguments with the people posting comments on the Facebook page (see Figure 2.2).

Figure 2.2   *Yowch!*

Where do I start? Obviously, you don't argue with your customers in an online forum. That's never okay.

But I think this leads to a bigger question: Who's running your social media campaigns? Just like you'd never let the PR intern issue a press release she wrote on behalf of the company, you also shouldn't let someone fresh out of school with no practical experience manage your social media campaigns. The problem is, for whatever reason, people aren't thinking like that.

Companies see *social media* and think *tech*, and when people think *tech*, they tend to think "the young kid who knows how to set up my iPad."

That's a costly, costly mistake. You need to make sure that the person running your social media campaign is also well-versed in interacting with the public. In fact, that's what social media is. You can't have someone who doesn't know how to keep up your image or brand. If you do, you'll lose.

Consider another example:

When a customer visited a Price Chopper store, he was relatively unhappy with his experience and he tweeted about it (see Figure 2.3).

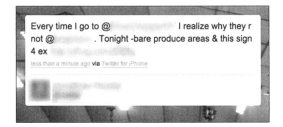

Every time I go to @   I realize why they r not @   . Tonight -bare produce areas & this sign 4 ex

less than a minute ago **via** Twitter for iPhone

Figure 2.3 *A common example of an unhappy customer.*

That happens. Life goes on, right? You'd respond and try to start a dialog, perhaps fix the person's problem, and turn a complainer into a fan. It's what we've talked about in the past, and it's a basic issue.

Except that that's not what happened here. A rogue employee didn't bother to reply. Instead, this employee contacted the original tweeter's *employer* and attempted to get the tweeter disciplined.

I'll pause here while you digest that.

Yeah. A little scary.

Obviously, that's *not* what you do.

The end result? The Price Chopper employee who contacted the customer's employer was made to apologize, she looked stupid, and the chain looked stupid by association. It's not something you want to do.

I know how annoying it can be to see someone posting something on the Web that you disagree with. If it's insulting to your company, your brand, your baby, every-thing into which you pour your heart and soul every day, then of course it's frus-trating as all hell to see someone—perhaps even some idiot, some *douche*, for lack of a better word—who has no ideas how much blood, sweat, and tears you put into your project come out and insult it.

And, yes, the first thing you feel like doing is ripping this idiot a new one, right through the same medium he used to call you out.

And I get that, and I understand why you'd want to.

But...

You can't.

You simply *have* to take the high road. You simply *have* to be the adult in the situation. You don't have a choice anymore. If you complain, if you snap back, or if you stoop to their level, as it were, then you're going to get burned. Nothing else matters—you will get burned.

Remember: anything you put online will be there forever. But more importantly, what you Direct Message or email is not private. If you call someone a jerk (even if the person *is* a jerk), that person has every reason to post your comments for all the world to see.

The following is a true story.

Someone was once trying to copy HARO. That's fine; information is free. The problem I had, though, was that he was blatantly stealing the code from my website and calling it his own. That's a problem.

My attorney sent him a cease-and-desist letter. He immediately scanned the letter and posted it online, trying to get more sympathy for his cause and trying to make me look like the big, evil meanie in the process.

However, what he wound up doing was further incriminating himself (he flat-out admitted he stole the code), but I also had to weather a mild storm of "wow, Peter is stifling competition" posts. Of course, none of that was true, and it was all posted by people with no understanding of the law. But, hey, that's what has to happen. People will always try to jump on the bandwagon. Your job is to ignore that.

End result, the storm quieted down, and I assume he found some other project on which to work.

And, yes, swallowing your anger and ignoring it simply sucks. But it has to be done.

Instead, be proactive. Reply in a constructive, proactive way. Engage the customer who hates you. If you try and he still doesn't do anything, so be it. But you have to try. You have to kill him with kindness, as it were. And it's doable. And once you've answered his question or complaint to the best of your ability, don't keep pushing it. Logical people will see what you've done, and they'll pay him less credence. You've answered the question in a mature, correct way.

Doing Something Is Better Than Doing Nothing

When you have a customer service or social media problem, the worst thing you can do—as I've talked about—is not do *anything*. That's even worse than...well, there's nothing worse than not doing anything. That's why it's the biggest problem.

Ever hear of Kryptonite Locks? Those big, heavy bike locks that are virtually unpickable? You know, except if you have a Bic pen (see Figure 2.4)? About two years ago, a video surfaced showing exactly how easy it was to pick these "unpickable" locks with nothing more than a 14-cent pen. And the video hit YouTube.

Figure 2.4   *Don't let a product disaster also turn into a social media disaster because you refuse to participate.*

And Kryptonite said nothing.

And it went viral. And hundreds of thousands of people looked at it.

Oops.

And Kryptonite said nothing.

And the news media picked up on it.

And, *finally*, Kryptonite said something.

The end result? Kryptonite had a $15 million recall on its hands. The company would have had that anyway. But, it also had a ton of bad press, bad PR, and bad marketing to contend with.

It wasn't like Kryptonite didn't see this coming. As soon as the first video posted, they could have gotten management, product development, tech, and customer service together with marketing and said something like, "We've got a problem here. It's not going to go away anytime soon. What do we do?"

They could have immediately issued a release to say they were looking into it. At least it would have been *something*. But they didn't. So instead of *just* having a $15 million recall on their hands, now they had a $15 million recall, as well as massively bad PR for a company who didn't say anything.

Ouch.

Anyone with a camera phone or BlackBerry can now be the next reporter breaking the next news story. Dell found that out the hard way when Gizmodo (www. gizmodo.com) broke a story about a Dell computer exploding—and posted video.

"We have video" is never what you want to hear.

Laptop explodes, Dell initially goes quiet, people freak, and hilarity ensues. Again— come forward first and talk about what's going on, and life goes on from there. Remaining silent hurts. A lot. A simple statement, such as "We know there's a problem and we're working on a solution" is better than saying nothing.

Your Audience Is Smarter Than You Are

By now, everyone in the world has seen video of what happens when you put a Mentos (those little candy/mint things) in a bottle of Coca-Cola. It explodes like Mount Vesuvius (see Figure 2.5).

Figure 2.5   *Wheeeee!*

However, when this was brought to Coke's attention, first they ignored it and then said, "Well, our soda is for drinking."

That didn't win them many friends.

Finally, they had to accept the fact that people were having a blast dunking little candies into sodas and causing ceiling stains the world over. So Coke finally did get into social media in a big way. Eventually, Coke came out in a roundabout way and said "Yes, our consumers control our brand."

The problem is, to this day, Coke is still playing catch-up ball to Pepsi products, who embraced social media from day one and have incorporated it into everything they do.

The list goes on and on and on. In the end, you need to remember that your brand is only as good as your customers perceive it to be—and your customers only perceive it to be good when it actually is.

One lesson worth learning: Never try to prove that you're smarter than your audience. Your audience is always smarter than you, and you have to remember and respect that.

Never Deceive Your Audience

With respect to that last point—that your audience is always smarter than you—I give you Wal-Mart. "Wal-Marting Across America" was a cute little blog run by a couple who drove an RV around the country, parking in Wal-Mart parking lots each night. It was the classic American success story: husband and wife decide to see this great land of ours, and Wal-Mart is where they choose to park their vehicle.

Great story, great "American" story, great press for Wal-Mart—which they ate up like it was a Mentos dipped in Coke.

Until one small thing happened.

Someone found out that the money for this trip? The idea for this trip? The funding for the RV and everything surrounding it? Well, it was kinda funded by...

Wait for it...

Wal-Mart.

Oops!

Yeah. That gave Wal-Mart one heck of a credibility problem, pretty dang quick.

It's one thing to embrace a popular story that seems to be gaining traction and help talk about it and grow it. It's another thing to lie about the entire story because *you made it up in the first place!*

And you're sitting there and saying, "Oh, that'll never happen to us. We don't do that. We can't afford an RV! We're not that big! That's not our problem!"

To which I might say the following:

Yes, you're right. You won't ever have an image problem like that because you won't ever buy an RV and fake a story.

But...

- What if an employee posts a review of one of your products somewhere online without admitting that he works for you and then gets caught?

- What if you have a download available on the iTunes store, and your PR agency, without telling you, has all its employees write favorable reviews?

- What if you write a letter to a blogger talking about this great product and conveniently forget to mention that, oh yeah, you work for the company that makes the product?

I can go on...but I shouldn't have to. The fact is, simply put:

Any and all forms of lying in any kind of forum that's at all open to the public will eventually come back to bite you in the ass.

Maybe not today, maybe not tomorrow, but eventually it will. And when it does, it will hurt. And when it hurts, you may be able to recover from it. You may not. But either way, it's going to be a lot more painful for you than if you hadn't done it in the first place. Make sense?

So, when it comes down to it, follow these four rules that I hammer in this book. They're quite simple, and worth repeating:

- **Be transparent.** Transparency rules the day, every time. Be honest, and you've got no lies to remember.

- **Be relevant to your audience.** The more in tune you are with how your audience likes to receive its information, the better off you'll be when you do have a problem. You'll be able to get to them quicker and more directly, and you'll have a better shot at getting your response out there and heard by the people who matter the most.

- **Be brief.** If you're in trouble, get to the point and fix the problem.

- **Finally, say *something*, and listen for feedback.** Remember: the companies that I've discussed in this chapter, and tons more like them, got in trouble for not listening, not responding, lying, or believing that they were smarter than their audiences. In the end, they were all proved wrong.

It's a fact of life in a social media world that you're going to have problems. Everyone does. Every company does. Expect them. Budget for them. It's something you have to do.

What you *don't* have to do, though, is make them worse. Don't lie. Don't blame. Don't ignore.

Work the problem, and find the solution. The quicker you do that, the quicker you can implement said solution, explain to your audience what happened, get past it, and move on.

Once you *do* move on, you can push forward with creating new and better fans. And because you're doing that, your next problem will be much less of a headache.

3

Before the Explosion: Winning Your Customer

The goal is to get, thrill, and keep the customer—in that order. Your job is to build your customer's loyalty to you long before you ever make the first sale and continue building it so the next customer comes on the first customer's recommendation.

Ever hear the phrase the tip of the iceberg? Supposedly, 90% of the iceberg is below the surface, where it can't be seen. People see a few hundred feet of ice in the ocean and assume that's all it is. What they don't see is the few thousand feet below the surface, extending down to the depths of the sea below.

Or, how about a skyscraper? Hundreds of stories tall (and a BASE jumper's dream) rising like a spire to the sky. But how come the wind doesn't tip it over and knock it all down like a house of cards? If you'd watched the skyscraper being built from the beginning, you'd notice that the first thing the workmen do is use heavy machinery to excavate the ground and then ram beams way into the earth, sometimes as far as hundreds of feet down.

What do icebergs and skyscrapers have in common? A strong, stable, and trustworthy foundation. The building doesn't get knocked down because the foundation extends hundreds of feet into the earth. The iceberg doesn't tip over because it has thousands of feet of ice balancing it below the water.

The strength of anything—a home, a family, a corporation, a building, anything—is almost entirely dependent on the strength of the foundation below.

In a world where social media is quickly becoming the norm, the same rule is true. Want to make sure you keep your customers when your company has a breakdown? You'd better make sure you've spent all your time up until that point building the most solid foundation possible. Want to use current customers to bring in new customers? Want to make customers so happy that they'll go and do your PR for you, without you even asking? (Customer-driven PR is the coolest form of PR there is.) In this chapter, we discuss how to do that in a few basic moves.

Before the Customer Is Even a Customer

When I was 14 and a freshman in high school, I remember my parents attending a "What to expect now that your kid is in high school" assembly the first week of school. And what I remember the most about it (other than the natural embarrassment a 14-year-old feels when in the presence of his parents) is that the guidance counselor, Dr. Wile, gave out his number to his private office line as he stood on the stage. He told something like 1,200 parents how to reach him, allowing them to bypass the switchboard, if they ever had a problem or needed to talk to him.

I remember that stuck with me—and with my parents, who wrote down his number, like the other 1,198 parents in attendance. He did something completely unexpected and quite beneficial. For my entire four years of high school, my parents remembered Dr. Wile—and obviously, 20 years later (ugh! 20 years!), so do I.

How can you be different before your customer is even a customer? Social media, being about customer service, is also about servicing the pre-customers. You want to reach them before they even know they need to buy from you and you alone.

One of the countless beauties of social media is that there are so many ways to start earning a good reputation long before the customer is a customer, when he just finds you for the first time on Google or—best of all—hears about you from a friend or trusted associate. (Get to know that term—*trusted associate*. As social media continues to become the norm rather than the exception, it's going to be the biggest link to you getting new customers and clients.)

So, if that's the case (and it is), it comes down to this: You have one goal right now, and that's to sell. However, you really need to have two goals at all times: To sell, and to do so in such a way that you make your customers feel like rock stars from the second they find you and for the rest of their lives.

Driving Revenue

I've said this before, and I'll continue to say it—social media for the sake of social media is pointless. If you really want to "own" this thing we call customer service in the social media world, you need to understand one thing: It has to drive revenue. It can drive revenue in any form:

- It can save money.

- It can earn money.

- It can bring in new clients who will spend money.

- It can cut costs and let you keep more of the money you're already earning.

But at the end of the day, customer service must generate revenue. End of story, case closed, go start the car.

Here's the ultimate, absolute kicker: Ready? It's really not so hard to do. Honestly. So, let's talk about it. How do we do it before they're even customers?

Find Out Where Your Customers Are

The First Rule: Before they're even customers, find out where the heck they are.

Casey Stengel, the manager of the 1969 New York Mets, was once asked how the team had such an amazing winning season. He thought for a second and then responded, "Well, we hit 'em [the baseball] where they [the opposing players] ain't." In other words, the Mets won ballgames by making sure to get hits. How did they get hits? By hitting the ball to places where the opposing team members weren't.

Your job is to do the opposite. Hit 'em where they are. So, before your customers are even customers, how do you use social media to find them?

The answer is simple: Know your customers before they're your customers by finding out where your current customers are. Creating a company page on LinkedIn won't do a lot for you if all of your current customers only use Facebook.

So, to paraphrase Casey Stengel: How do you find potential new customers and convert them into current customers? "Hit 'em where they are." Find your current audience's hangouts, and start there.

But, that raises several questions: in a world full of fractured media—where people have multiple options to receive their email each day in different formats, genres, and paths—how do you know how to reach them? How do you find the right way to contact them? Where should you go to make sure your audience is not only receiving your information, but also responding to it and acting on it?

In other words, how do you know where to reach your oh-so-coveted audience?

The answer is surprisingly simple: Ask your audience how they like to get their information.

How does your audience like to get their information? Twitter and Facebook? A podcast and an RSS feed? The *New York Times* and *BusinessWire*? Telegraph? Whichever way they choose to get their information, you'd better know. And you'd better make sure you're doing regular updates to see if anything's changed.

If you're just getting your feet wet in the social media space, talk to your most trusted clients and customers. Ask them where they go. Ask them where they hang out online. (You'll see several repetitive themes here—asking is way, way underrated.) You want to know where your best customers spend their time. Why? Because that's probably where your *potential* customers are, as well.

Take good notes. The information you get from your best customers will be goldmines. Here are some questions to ask your best customers:

- How did they first find out about you?

- Where do they spend most of their time online?

- Do they use social networking? In what capacity?

- What kind of mobile phone do they have? (You think this is too nitty-gritty? Well, if for some reason, 85% of your audience DOES NOT carry a smartphone, investing in mobile campaigns might be jumping the gun and a waste of money right now.)

- Where does your audience hang out online?

- Where does your audience hang out offline?

- How would your audience prefer you communicate with them? (This is an important question—the answers from this alone, if appropriately understood and used, can double or triple your sales overnight.)

- How socially active are your customers online? Unless you're selling party equipment, you don't need to know how socially active they are, well, socially.)

And so on, and so on. If they're truly your best customers, ask them and they'll be willing to share. Don't bombard them, but get some information out of them. Then look at that info. Are you seeing patterns?

- Are most of them on Facebook? Twitter? LinkedIn? Foursquare?

- Do they prefer email?

- Do they have smartphone devices?

- Do they text? Email? Both?

- Do they have kids? (Ask this because, if they don't know how to use the features of their new smartphone they got for Christmas, their kids surely do.)

- Or, by chance, are they part of the 21% of the United States that's NOT on the Internet?

This is the kind of data you want and the kind of information you can use to start building your customers' social profiles. That social profile will enable you to target the right areas and get to the right places. For you, those right places are, simply like Casey said, where they are.

Chances are, where your customers currently are is the place you're going to start finding new ones. So that's the first rule: Hit 'em where they are.

Pay Attention

The second rule: Listen.

I don't think anyone would argue that right now, the number-one real-time social media listening device is Twitter, with Facebook a close second and closing the gap daily. The ability to listen to your audience (or your competitors' audiences) in real time, as they complain, compliment, or just talk in general terms about your industry is unprecedented. Take full advantage of it.

Use the free tools at your disposal to listen in: Tweetdeck is one of the best and easiest ways to listen to multiple conversations about multiple topics in real time.

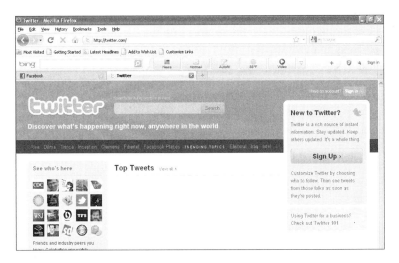

Figure 3.1   *The Home Page of Twitter at http://twitter.com*

Head to Facebook and start searching for your company name and for your competitors' names. Don't forget to include popular misspellings!

Use Google alerts (http://news.google.com) to find the same things in the blogosphere, as well as what you might have missed when you were sleeping or not paying attention. (Face it, we all have to watch http://www.tmz.com at some point in our day. It can't all be work.)

From a simple glance on Tweetdeck, Google, or Twitter, I can see who's talking about my company, who's mentioning my name, who's talking about my industry, and what the hot trending topics currently are. It's quite easy, and I can leave it running on my desktop, glancing at it a few times an hour for a few seconds at a time. There's literally no easier way to take an immediate pulse of any topic in which you might be interested, professionally, personally, or otherwise.

What are potential customers saying? Are they complaining about the way a competitor does business? If so, is there a way to engage them and turn them into customers for you? (We discuss this later in the book.)

WORKING WITH—INSTEAD OF AGAINST— THE MEDIA

Perhaps you hear current or potential customers talking about something in your industry that could be considered a trend. If that's the case, why not write it up in a few paragraphs, explaining what you think the trend is, and send it off to a reporter you know who covers your industry? What better way to a) make friends and b) get a story mentioning your company? And, of course, we all know what happens when you get a story with a positive mention of your company—you get new customers! Wowza! (Added bonus? You're now the first company to "discover" this trend. You're über-cool! Reporters will call you directly from now on! Score!)

Like any construction worker or contractor, you want to use the tools that work best for the situation in which you find yourself.

Let's go back to the first rule for a second (finding out where your customers are): Once you know where your audience is, it's a lot easier to reach them.

Again, we should go back and remember the "ask your current customers questions" rule. They're already your customers! Asking them a question or two won't hurt! In fact, it'll help. (I bring that up again because it's relevant again, and it always will be.)

It could be something as simple as, "Are you on Facebook?" Or perhaps, "Do you tweet?" Afraid to even go there? Ask them simply, "How do you get your information?" They'll talk. Trust me, they'll talk. Simple questions like that will tell you where your audience is. Stop asking people for their home numbers. Ask for their mobile numbers, and only their mobile numbers. Ask them if they text. (Betcha they do.) Find out if they use any GPS on their devices.

Consider it covert ops. But know that you don't have to be covert about it at all. So, I guess you could consider it...ops. Just ops. Tell all your employees as well. There's nothing wrong with everyone asking the occasional question or two. Good operatives ask questions. That's what they do. Haven't you ever watched a James Bond movie? Villains (and for that matter, customers) just *love* to talk. It makes them feel important. Why do you think James Bond always gets out of those sticky situations? Because the villain has some random need to tell Mr. Bond exactly how he's going to kill him, what he's going to do once Bond is dead, and how he's going to escape.

The REALLY smart wanna-be worldwide dominators and psychopaths would be smart to just shut the heck up once in a while, no? But anyway, I digress. Ask your customers questions, and get them talking. And, hey—taking notes every once in a while wouldn't hurt, either.

Devise a Plan to Reach Your Customers

The third rule: Once you know where your customers are, devise a plan to get them.

There's a survivalist named Les Stroud. He used to have a TV show called *Survivorman*, on which he'd go out into the jungle, or a snow-covered tundra, or the top of a mountain. He'd be there, all alone, for one week, having to film the entire ordeal himself. Totally fun show. The part I loved the most, though, was how he always managed to make things out of nothing. He'd be in the hottest spot in Africa, yet he'd find a way to make water out of sand. And the coolest thing was that he'd show you what he was doing, so you could do it, too! You know, just in case you ever randomly found yourself in the hottest spot in Africa. I usually find myself at my local pizza shop, but if the whole place ever just randomly turned to sand, I'd be set for water, thanks to *Survivorman*.

Point being, you can't just find your audience and then walk to where they are and start talking to them. You have to have a plan. You have to do something I call *LLR*: Listen, listen, react.

You want to listen to your audience, then listen to the response your audience gets, and then react with something that provides value to both parties. Some quick examples and lessons follow:

Example: When a passenger complained via Twitter about Airline A making an unscheduled landing at an unexpected destination with no valid way to get the passenger home that day, the airline could have listened and immediately reacted. They didn't. In fact, they didn't say anything at all. They stayed silent, reacting by not reacting and ignoring the pleas of the customer. Airline B listened to the complaining customer, listened for a reaction from the Airline A, and when they didn't hear one offered the customer a flight leaving an hour later—at no cost. The customer is now a huge fan of Airline B, tells everyone who will listen how great they are, and travels a few hundred thousand miles on Airline B each year. Quite the financial windfall for Airline B. How could Airline A have staved off such a poach? By listening and responding. They did neither, and Airline B has a new customer. Perhaps more importantly, Airline A doesn't have that customer anymore.

Lesson: To grow, listen, and respond.

Example: When a restaurant in the Midwest saw more and more of its current customers using a new geo-location game called Foursquare, they hopped on the bandwagon to figure out what it was all about. They discovered that their best customers were coming to their restaurants more often than those who didn't use the game. Those customers were visiting often to gain "status" on the game at this particular restaurant. So, the restaurant threw its own prizes into the mix and attracted more customers than it ever thought possible.

Lesson: To try something new, listen, and respond.

Example: When a small flower shop wanted to drum up some new business, they created a Facebook fan page and encouraged their current customers to post their best reasons for giving or receiving flowers. When they posted, each fan was given a code to use for a few dollars off his next flower purchase. Some of the stories written were so good that they got passed around —and each one had the flower store name included. Result? New customers through old customers.

Lesson: To build, listen, and respond.

So now they're your customers....

Congratulations! They've bought something! That's always a nice feeling. But now what? Just because they're customers doesn't mean they'll stick around. Remember that other companies sell the same things you do. You've got to be better.

Following are some additional ideas for reaching your customer:

As the Sale Is Happening

Remember the rule listen, listen, react. Ask questions. Are you on Twitter? Do you use Facebook? Would you care to follow us/fan us? One online store will automatically deduct a dollar from your order if you become a fan on Facebook. How do they do that? They have a new coupon code each day on the fan page. If you go to the fan page and enter it, it takes a dollar off the price. That's an easy way to gain some valuable insight about your new client while adding a fan. Additionally, it makes the customer happier because she saved a buck!

I know a small bottled water company that personally includes thank-you notes written by the packers for each new customer the first time they buy their water. It's just a quick note, explaining how they're happy to have them as a customer and look forward to serving them again in the future, but it makes a world of difference.

Zappos almost always upgrades to free overnight shipping on a customer's first order. Why? Because they want you back, and they want you happy, and they want you sharing those emotions!

A diamond dealer started giving out little flip-cams (www.theflip.com) to his best customers to let them record the look on their wife's or girlfriend's face when they opened up the small little box. He posted some online and got rave reviews. The cost? Each camera is about $100.

What can you do—what *little thing* can you do—to make a customer happy that they purchased from you? Remember that happy customers talk online second only to unhappy customers. You want to tip the scales in your favor.

Customer service has changed dramatically thanks to social media. Now more than ever, the little things matter even more than the big things because it's easy to get people to talk about the little things for you.

Right now—as you're reading this—come up with three little changes that don't cost you much (if any) money that you can implement today to make your customers smile and talk about what a nice surprise they received from you. Go ahead. I'll wait.

I can implement the following ideas right now:

1)

2)

3)

SeamlessWeb.com, an online food delivery service in several major cities, lets you tweet your order right after you buy it. "I'm starving, but getting Ray's Pizza delivered, thanks to Seamless Web!" You know they can monitor who's tweeting when and back it right up.

If your customer is ordering online, it's easy to put a "tweet this!" button next to the order. People love to share when they buy stuff—perhaps it makes them less likely to regret spending the money.

Once the Sale Is Complete

Mom always told me to write a thank-you note. I hated them, but what an impression they made. Thank-you notes are great for countless reasons. They make you think of the person sending them, sometimes a few weeks after the initial transaction. They're a physical object that is received via mail, yet almost no one sends them anymore. Today? The mail is primarily bills and junk. All the real stuff happens on email. Or does it?

What would happen if, every time a new customer bought from you, you sent a thank-you card to her? Not after every purchase, but the first time. What if the card had a code for 10% off the second purchase, as a thank you?

Every time I call my concierge at American Express for something, I get a follow-up email a few days letter asking how what they did for me was. Did I enjoy the dinner they reserved? Did my mom like the flowers they sent?

They're always striving for improvement. You can, too. Doing so will result in repeat visitors and word-of-mouth action.

If the product is physical in nature, ask for photos of it in action! Tifosi makes really nice sports sunglasses. After I received a pair, they emailed me to invite me to submit photos of me wearing the sunglasses during a race. I did, and it made the front page of their fan page. It didn't take long to do, and everyone got a little happier from the experience. Check them out here: http://3.ly/EyNT

I'm a huge fan of SportBeans, which are jelly beans designed for people who do strenuous workouts—adventure racers, marathoners, triathletes, and so on. When I signed up to complete my first Ironman, I knew I'd have a lot of training ahead of me. So I emailed SportBeans, told them I kept a blog where I wrote about my training, and asked if I could somehow get them involved.

Two emails later, four huge boxes of SportBeans showed up, along with racing shirts, a cap, and a few water bottles.

SportBeans fan for LIFE, yo! And think about this: not only do they get the knowledge that I'm going to tweet about it (which I did) or mention it on Facebook (which I did), but I also now have clothing to wear during my race. And, of course, what happens as I race? Photos get taken, which get uploaded to my blog and to Facebook and to friends' Facebook pages. And they now all have giant SportBeans logos floating across the middle of their pages. Not bad as a result of my email, is it?

And by the way, other companies who are doing this right are listening to what their competitors are doing. What does this mean? It means they're doing it and you're not. If I could wag my finger at you through this book, you know I'd be doing it right now. Come on, now. No one likes to have a finger wagged at them. So to avoid that, here are a few more examples of things you can do to trounce your competition and assume that first customer becomes a customer for life and, more importantly, *does your PR for you!*

I showed up at a Sheraton Hotel a little while back and found waiting for me in my room not just the regular "here's a bottle of water" that one would normally get, but a plate of fruit and a few PowerBars. Why? Because someone at the Sheraton Overland Park in Kansas City had taken the time to research me. I'm one of their most loyal customers, but they went above and beyond. They found that I had a blog at www.shankman.com and had mentioned that I was training for an Ironman. The Sheraton included a note saying how much they like my blog and if I needed anything, to call them. Check it here: http://twitter.com/petershankman/statuses/14734644857.

That blew my mind. So the first thing I did was tweet about how spectacular that hotel was. I mean, come on, they read my blog!!

Ask yourself this question:

With the information your new customer has given you, what can you do to make that customer feel special? What can you to do make this transaction "the transaction of the day" for him?

I'll take it a step further. What kind of *homework* can you do on your client before he even buys/steps foot in/checks in/walks through the door/makes the purchase? What can you tell him about him? And not in a creepy-stalker kind of way, either!

I know a woman who runs a shopping service for men. When a man calls her looking for the perfect gift for his wife, not only does she help, but she also sends a "top-ten-ways-not-to-screw-up-your-anniversary" PDF file that she wrote a long time ago. The article is written tongue-in-cheek, and all of her customers get a kick out of it. A lot of them forward it to their friends, and of course, on the bottom, is her website and contact info.

Can you write a quick article that you can send out as a "pre-thank-you?"

There's a restaurant in Manhattan I go to from time to time. Not a lot, and I'm certainly not what they'd call a frequent diner. But one day, I walked in and there was quite a line. I mentioned to my friend that we should go somewhere else and started to turn away. The person behind the desk came over to us when he noticed we were leaving and said, "Hey guys, there's a bit of a wait, but why don't you have a drink at the bar on us? What's your name? We'll let you know when a table is ready."

It cost them the price of a drink, but it kept us there for dinner and made us loyal. We go there more often now. That, of course, leads to better treatment and recognition, which is what we all desire, anyway. What do you desire? Can you give it to your customers? Chances are, they desire it, too.

You want that first customer to "go loyal" from the second she walks in. Customers who "go loyal" are more likely to blog, post, Facebook, and so on and are more likely to become influencers for their friends. You want to spot the person in the group to whom all the others turn for questions and advice. Treat that person well, and she'll do your PR for you. And again, that's your goal—both online and off.

Think really hard. You know this has happened to you in the past. The key is remembering how you felt at that point and turning it around so your customers feel the same way.

Remember how you felt when you got your last airline upgrade? Or when you got the free drink or someone got you in without waiting in line? Remember how you wanted to tell people that so fast and share it with the world? Welcome to that world—you can do that now. Social media will get it there. And you don't even have to ask your customers or clients to do it. They'll *want* to do it to simply show how well they were treated!

Look around and ask everyone near you to raise their hands if they DON'T have a camera installed in their phone.

Note crickets.

Or worse, you probably aren't even reading this book around other people. You are alone; in front of your computer; or reading this on a Kindle, an iPad, or an iPhone. Okay, if that's the case, post it in your status, "Hey, @petershankman wrote this book I'm reading and he asked everyone to tell if they don't have a camera in their phone. Anyone reading this NOT have a camera in their phone?"

Then watch no one comment.

So, if everyone's walking around with a camera in their phone and a way to transmit, then that means that everyone's a journalist. And if everyone's a journalist, then everyone has to be treated like a journalist.

And I pretty much guarantee you that if Larry King or Bill O'Reilly walked into your restaurant, you'd give him a free drink while you cleared a table.

Do you have to do that for everyone? Of course not. But simply "reacting nicer" is one of the easiest ways to go about starting that shift.

"Sitting at the bar, having a drink because my table isn't ready" could easily turn into "Sitting at TaCocina; they just gave me a free drink because my reservation was delayed! Sweet!"

When was the last time you heard anyone say "Sweet!" in conjunction with "My reservation was delayed!" Win!

Even the simplest things can make the biggest differences. The thank-you card is one example: "Thank you, @petershankman, for becoming part of the <company name> family." I don't care how big your company is, you're not so automated that you can't figure out a way to thank your new customers. This is how you turn them into fans for life.

Case Studies

Following are a pair of case studies illustrating the points I've made in this chapter.

Solemates.com

SoleMates—http://www.thesolemates.com/

Solemates is a small, two-year-old company that produces items that women stick on the bottom of their high-heeled shoes to prevent them from sinking into the grass when they're at garden parties or outdoor weddings. Recently, the company took all fulfillment in-house, as opposed to outsourcing it. This allows Solemates to send little notes of congratulations in the box each time they know they're sending a wedding party order. From this simple act, they've seen their referral orders increase dramatically.

How can you continue to make these little differences, resulting in big increases in sales and revenue?

Here's a simple example of SoleMates' website navigation bar. Note the Facebook and Twitter links on the bottom. It's simple, easy, and—most importantly—inviting.

React when your audience reaches out—Whether it's a purchase, a question, or a comment. Check it out:

Figure 3.2   *Adding social media links to your site is easy.*

HARO

Every time an advertisement is purchased on the HARO mailing list (about three or four times a day), I get a quick email to my BlackBerry, set up with the person's name, email, and what he bought. It takes less than 10 seconds to see his name, click on his email, and compose my own email to him saying, "Hey, thanks for buying a HARO ad! Any questions or problems, let me know!"

What does this do? Well, automatically, it makes the customer happy about his decision to purchase from me. Almost immediately after he has spent $1,500, $3,000, or as much as $18,000 on HARO advertising, he gets an immediate (not automatic!) email from the CEO of the company. This is personal. This is REAL. This instantly puts him at ease.

Plus, now he has a personal (not a corporate) contact at HARO, and it doesn't get any higher-level than the CEO. Does he have a problem? He knows he can come to me, and even if I pass it off to a subordinate, the customer knows he'll be taken care of.

This is how you achieve loyal, almost rabid, fans willing to tell the world, without any prompting, how great you are. HARO is living proof. It works every day, sometimes multiple times a day.

And what does it take from me? Just a BlackBerry and the willingness to quickly send a 10-second email. I don't care how many customers you have or how busy you are.

Rule: WE ALL HAVE TEN SECONDS.

We can all send those kinds of emails. And we can do them personally, and we can make our new customers loyal immediately. That's the goal, and that's harnessing the power of social media.

What will it take for you?

Customer Service Is a Way of Life

Story time. As I was getting my notes together to write this chapter, I was sitting in London Heathrow Airport, waiting for my flight back to New York. Sitting down with my headphones on, lost in my own little world, I looked up to see a man next to me having trouble connecting via Wi-Fi to the airport network. To save him some trouble, I opened up a port on my portable wireless network and instructed him on how to use it. He got online, and I didn't think twice about it.

Halfway through my flight, I looked up from my seat to find him standing over me. He'd looked at my laptop and had seen my HARO sticker on it. He had then Googled me to find out who I was. Turns out, he runs communications for a very large oil utility with locations worldwide. And what do you know, he was looking for a person or agency to help his company get a handle on this whole "social media" thing. We exchanged cards, and I had a new client.

Here's the kicker, though: before he came over to me (he knew he had at least seven hours in flight), he looked me up online. He searched "HARO." From there, he found http://helpareporter.com. And from there, he found me as CEO with a photo. He then Googled my name and found http://shankman.com. The first icon he clicked there was "speaking," which showed him several speaking clips from various conferences at which I've spoken. From there, he looked up other clients I had, one click away under "Clients." Finally, he read a few recent blog posts I'd posted.

He told me that he came over to talk to me only after reading about me and finding out about me online. "Random nice guy helping him out" wouldn't have cut it for a first conversation.

My online presence got me a new, very well-funded client.

Will yours?

See, it all ties in. Brand is really just a made-up word that means everywhere. Everything you do, everywhere you are, every place you go, everything seen around you—it's all a part of your brand. Whether it's online or offline, whether it's in person or via a digital image, it's all about leaving everyone—the customer, the client, the guy next to you at the airport—with the feeling that if they don't get to know you, your company, or your brand, they're missing out.

That's customer service, right there. It's not just a thing to do, and social media isn't just a way to do it. It's a way of life. It's not something you can just do when you feel like it.

But on the same note, don't let it freak you out. This doesn't mean you need to devote every waking second to social media, thereby forgetting about your real job. It doesn't mean you need to check in with a mobile device every single time you step outside your home or office, and it doesn't mean you need to post every photo that's taken of you or every story you read.

It simply means you need to be aware.

Part of customer service now means being aware. It means you have to listen to what's out there and act accordingly. You need to have a strong foundation and grow your business one customer at a time. It also means you get to have fun.

I mean, come on—if you're not having fun with this thing we call life, then seriously, what is the point?

So....Are you inspired yet?

No? How about this:

Ninety percent of people say that they trust recommendations of their friends over advertisements. That's not a shock (at least it shouldn't be), but if that's the case, then your job is to get recommended to those 90% of people by your customers!

I'm putting together cycling jerseys for my cycling team. I did some online research and saw 15 different sites that all claim to be the best. I went on Twitter, and got 10 recommendations, including photos of the jerseys that were made. End of the day? I chose a recommendation by someone I trusted. As would you.

Here's another statistic: 38% of people follow brands to get product updates, but more than 60% of those same people would go to the brand on Twitter if they couldn't resolve a problem through customer service.

I doubt these stats are shocking to you. I also don't think they're that out of the ordinary. In fact, if anything, they're surprisingly low. And by the time this book winds up in your hands, they'll most likely be higher.

So, what does that mean? It means you have to act. Again, that shouldn't be a shock. But perhaps even now, several chapters into this book, you might be asking yourself, "So how do I start?"

Go call five customers. Seriously. Go call five customers. They can be customers who like you or customers who you've never talked to before. Just spend the next 20 minutes getting five customers on the phone. Ask them, in order, the following:

1. *What's the number-one online social media outlet you use to get your information?*

2. *Where do you place the most trust from recommendations?*

3. *Do you read any newspapers? Which one(s)?*

4. *How did you first find out about us?*

5. *Is there anything, off the top of your head, that we can do better?*

Ask those five questions to five customers, and you have the start of your social media plan. I'm serious! Let's examine, for example, the first question: "What's the number-one online social outlet you use to get your information?"

Ask this question of five people, and, chances are, you'll hear one answer more frequently than the others. If you've done absolutely nothing with social media whatsoever, the answer you hear most is a good place to start. Whether it's Facebook, Twitter, The NY Times Blog, or even something you've never heard of, get in there and start exploring. Go wander around the site. You won't break it. Here's a fun challenge: Create an account and then see who else you know on the site. We do this with lawyers all the time to break down their built-in barriers to social networking. When they find that more than 75% of their peers are online, they get much, much less abject to using it.

Let's say it's Facebook. Go online. Create an account. Add a few photos. Offer 10% off to the first 20 people who "fan" you. Tell some customers, and see if they "fan" you. Then see what happens when they do. Let them submit content, or ask them to. See what they've got. Choose a winner, and give that person another discount.

Congratulations. You now have a social media program.

Look at what Dalch Wellness, a holistic wellness company with clients nationwide, does on its Facebook fan page (see Figure 4.1). One person runs the site, and the entire company. Yet she finds the time to update the page every day with something simple and quick, and it draws in fans.

Figure 4.1 *Dalch Wellness has the right idea for a Facebook fan page.*

By asking a simple question each day, the company is able to increase interaction with its fans and grow its business. It's simple. It takes five seconds, and it has the makings of a decent social media program that can grow as the company does. That's it! We're not curing disease here! Well, technically, I suppose Dalch Wellness could be, but still....

Here's an easy example of how one small restaurant could grow its business by cross-breeding local, on-the-street, smart marketing with social media.

Let's say there's a small bakery outside Central Park in New York. Lots of people run in Central Park, every single day.

What if this small bakery decided, because it's open at 5:30 a.m. for all the early risers who like to get coffee anyway, to put out a giant 5-gallon dispenser of water and little mini-cups each morning? They could put a little doggie bowl down on the ground next to it, as well.

It would cost the bakery the total cost of the dispenser and cups—perhaps a few bucks a week. People walking by would see the free water, as would everyone walking home after their runs in Central Park. (Or, if they're like me, their lumber through Central Park.)

Anyway...in the past, this would be a strictly word-of-mouth event. People would hear about it, and perhaps they'd buy a cookie to celebrate their run when it was over. It was slow-moving at best, but it was all we had.

Nowadays, you can help that along.

Any idea how many running groups there are in your hometown? A lot. Any idea how many of them have Facebook pages? A lot.

What would it take for you to become a fan of all of them and shoot an email to the owner of the page (don't post on their wall because that's blatant self-promotion)? All it would take is just a short note that reads:

"Hey – You guys practice right by my bakery – Just want to let you know that we have a five-gallon dispenser of ice-cold water available all the time, from 5am to 10pm, outside the store. Always full, always free. You don't have to buy anything, just come grab some water after your hard workouts.

Happy training!

All the best, store owner name, store name."

That's it. Simple and to the point. You're not advertising or selling anything. You're not promoting yourself. You're helping.

Self-Promotion Versus Helping

RULE: Self-promotion, when done right, isn't self-promotion. It's *help*. I've mentioned this before. What can you do to help? What can you do to help the people who have yet to hear about you?

Remember, at its most basic form, social media *is help*. It's getting your message out there in such a way that it helps other people. This, in turn, allows other people to rely on you and, more to the point, *recommend you* when others ask for help. You become the helper.

You *want* to be the helper.

Helpers rule. Helpers make the rules, in fact.

Be the helper.

It can be something simple. How many times last week did someone send you something cool? What happens if you like it, and think others will, and repost it? That's the sharing of information. You've entered the world of sharing information, and people love that.

Figure 4.2 shows an example from my blog this morning, in which I made a quick post thanking Cadbury (the chocolate company) for posting an awesome commercial about a flying ostrich, to which I totally related. (I related because it's about people having to be themselves, not because I'm an ostrich.)

Within minutes, it was reposted, linked to, and otherwise passed around. What did I get out of it? Nothing. I shared the joy.

I also built the base. The more good stuff I share, the more people are willing to assume that what I post is smart and worthwhile. In a way, everything we post is building that base.

But it's also possible that things we post are taking away from that base. Post enough stuff without merit, or stuff not worthy of people's time, and you'll lose them. So understand your audience, and post appropriately.

And by the way: Watch the ostrich video. I dare you not to smile:

http://shankman.com/thank-you-cadbury-for-creating-this-commercial/

If you really haven't smiled, email me—I'll tell you some bad jokes from the Borscht Belt.

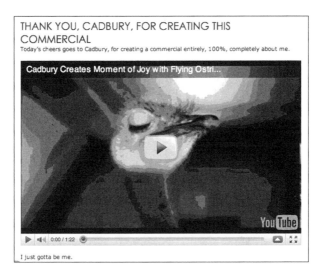

Figure 4.2   *An Ostrich, a smile, and all of a sudden, you forget it's actually an advertisement!*

Case Study: Bravo! Italian Restaurant and Bar

Check out what a high-end Italian restaurant in Jackson, Mississippi, did, as told to me by their business advisor, Marianna Chapman:

> "We have a client who showed me his numbers last week for a high-end, high-touch Italian restaurant in the Jackson, Mississippi, market. Bravo! Italian Restaurant and Bar has used Facebook and Twitter over the past year and during the same period drastically scaled back or completely eliminated all forms of traditional marketing. Their Facebook page allows customers to buy gift cards straight from Facebook, and one of their most successful campaigns was one where customers were asked to give a Bravo! to anyone deserving of a thank-you in the community by posting it right on the Facebook page.
>
> At the end of the nomination period, the Bravo! team voted for the most poignant thank-you and gave that person a $200 gift certificate. Best of all, the owner then went back—as an unannounced bonus—and sent smaller gift cards to each and every person who nominated someone else throughout the one-week campaign. To do this, he sent a personal message through Facebook to every single person who nominated—which was nearly 100 folks! This human touch and goodwill resulted in a huge increase in engagement on the Facebook page as well as an immediate boost in sales that continues to this day. Last month, Bravo! was up 21% in sales over last year and year-to-date comparisons (which was the month they started social media one year ago), they are up nearly 19%. Connect with Bravo!: www.facebook.com/bravobuzz and www.twitter.com/bravobuzz and the owner of the restaurant at www.twitter.com/JeffGoodBRAVO."

See? As we've said before: It's all about listening.

Case Study: Risdall Integration Group

Here's some more proof, thanks to Jared Roy, at the Risdall Integration Group:

> "Urban Bean Coffee is an independent coffee shop in Minneapolis. Within a 5-mile range of their coffee shop are 10 other coffee shops, including two Starbucks and one Caribou Coffee. It is a very competitive area for coffee shops. Last year, Roy Advertising worked with Urban Bean Coffee to start listening to Twitter conversations within 5 miles of their ZIP code for people talking about drinking their morning coffee as well as stopping into Starbucks, Caribou, and the other coffee shops in the area.

If someone mentions on Twitter, for example, that they just stopped in and grabbed their morning latte at Starbucks, Urban Bean reaches out to them and invites them to come over, saying they will buy them their drink of choice. Urban Bean also monitors people checking in on Foursquare to these coffee shops as well for outreach. They have been able to convert 35% of these customers into regulars. You can imagine the increased revenue this brings in when an average specialty coffee costs around $5. Urban Bean also offers a free cup of coffee to the Mayor on Foursquare to their location."

Check out what else Urban Bean is doing on its website: http://www.urbanbeancoffee.com/index.html

Think about it: Urban Bean is competing against Starbucks and Caribou! That's massive, yet it has managed to do it and make some stellar gains simply by listening, reacting, and making its audience feel special.

Getting any ideas yet? Starting to see how these little practical changes can generate revenue, increase sales, and move product?

Again, it's not like traditional marketing and advertising have to go away. But, if you can save a fortune on the traditional ways of doing things by bringing in new audiences and increasing sales using social media, why wouldn't you?

More importantly, why wouldn't you take what you learned in the traditional way of doing things and apply them to your new way of doing things? Don't forget the past if you can include it in new ways of doing good things in the future.

Case Study: Law Offices of Daniel R. Rosen, PC

Want more? How about a personal injury law firm? You know, one of those law firms that always advertise on TV? "Law firms?" you ask. But *they* can't use social media! But you'd be wrong. Check it....

Background

The Law Offices of Daniel R. Rosen, PC, is a personal injury firm with offices throughout Colorado, including Denver, which is the biggest market in the state. The firm specializes in all kinds of accident cases, but car and motorcycle accidents are its bread and butter.

The personal injury law market is extremely competitive. A major U.S. city such as Denver could have dozens or even hundreds of personal injury firms all competing for a limited number of clients.

The Law Offices of Daniel R. Rosen's ongoing marketing efforts, including phone book ads, TV commercials, and even newer initiatives such as PPC advertising, were becoming completely ineffective. So, they knew they needed to make a change fast. And with no marketing department and a meager budget compared to some of the huge law firms they were competing with, they knew they needed a more innovative (and cost-effective) way to make a splash.

A New Approach

So they shifted gears altogether. Instead of focusing on advertising, they decided to focus on sharing value. They created the Colorado Accident Law Blog to provide motorcycle safety tips, recent Colorado accident news, and a wealth of other information that would directly relate to their target audience—people injured in accidents anywhere in Colorado.

The Colorado Accident Law Blog isn't a legal blog written by a lawyer. Rather, it's a news blog written by a professional journalist and, as such, all the content is relevant, newsworthy, well-written, and search-optimized.

From Invisible to the First Page

Before the firm started blogging, it was completely invisible online. You couldn't find it on the first 10 pages of Google for any relevant keywords. After a newly designed website and just 6 weeks of blogging every day, the firm hit the first page of Google for "motorcycle accident Colorado," one of its most important search phrases.

Now, just over 3 months into blogging, the firm is on the first page of Google for "accident injury lawyer Denver," "accident injury lawyer Colorado," "motorcycle accident Colorado," "motorcycle accidents Colorado," and "Colorado personal injury accident lawyer," among others.

Since the firm began blogging, Google has accounted for nearly 60% of site visits; traffic is growing consistently; and dozens of comments, contact form submissions, phone calls, and emails are coming in from site visitors—many of them prospective clients.

Case Study: Grasshopper

Creating and sharing meaningful, relevant content can do more for a small business than any SEO or advertising campaign ever could. Remember that!

I found Grasshopper when they started advertising to small businesses on HARO. I asked its director of marketing for some more background on what he does with social media. With the exception of the FedEx campaign, everything that follows cost virtually nothing:

1. Created and sustained conversations from a branding campaign:

   • Anonymously FedExed 25,000 chocolate-covered grasshoppers to influential people and brought them online with an emotional viral video.

   • Used social media to "egg people on," to eat the grasshoppers and send in user-generated content. They got hundreds of pictures and videos of office personnel and children eating the grasshoppers, and they got eight national news anchors to eat them on-air during morning shows.

   • Grasshopper had fun with people and, because of social media, they kept the conversations going for nearly 3 months, instead of dying off in 1 week like most creative campaigns. I paid my assistant, Meagan, 50 bucks to eat a grasshopper on camera. Google "Meagan, grasshopper, Shankman" without the quotes.

   • They engaged the likes of Guy Kawasaki, Kevin Rose, Jason Calacanis, Mashable, and so on.

2. Grasshopper used social media to meet and promote their customers (creating brand loyalists!):

   • Anytime a customer tweets or engages Grasshopper positively via social media, the company reaches out to them and tries to make a connection offline. Clearly this customer is vocal, so Grasshopper spends 30 minutes learning about his business, his journey, and how they can help him.

   • Grasshopper has the customer fill out a "Tell Us Your Story" form, (http://grasshopper.com/tellusyourstory), which allows them to learn about what makes the customer unique and liter-ally get customers press.

   • Grasshopper averages at least one press story a month for customers and tons of connections.

3. Grasshopper launched an all-Twitter campaign and petition for a National Entrepreneurs' Day:

   • They engaged the first U.S. President on Twitter.

   • Grasshopper raised a ton of awareness around needing a day for entrepreneurs to be truly appreciated and rallied tons of influ-entials (all via social media).

Not bad for virtually zero cost. And according to Meagan, the Grasshopper was surprisingly tasty.

Case Study: Peter Kuhn's Food Truck

Several of the best ideas I heard of came after I tweeted that I was looking for good case studies on social media in small business and customer service.

Peter Kuhn replied and said that he's in the process of starting a food truck. (How cool is that?!) Here's what he sent me, word for word. I've italicized the really, really smart parts:

> "I am currently in the process of co-launching a Food Truck in Philly. The chef I am co-launching with is chef Tyson Wong Ophaso. Tyson has opened/owned and operated dozens of restaurants in New York, Philadelphia, LA, and Las Vegas. Together, he and I are building this small business in Philly with the hopes of getting back to the true roots of the culinary arts—to make people happy through the power of great/healthy food. You are a busy man, and I don't want to waste your time, so I will get into the specific character of the truck later. For now, I'll focus on how I use the social experience to grow and cultivate our online image.

> The utilities that I use most are Facebook, followed closely behind by Twitter. Combined, they are an incredible duo allowing me to *actively see our demographic and engage the audience in active, interesting dialogue.* For example, [we're] showing the progress of our merchandising design, our collaboration with a local clothing boutique/art gallery in our branding design, collaborative work with a popular Philly artist who is designing and painting the images wrapping our truck, and pictures of delightful new food our chef puts together. By sourcing the power of Facebook and Twitter, *I'm able to post rich content, for free, that people who anticipate the opening of the truck find interesting.* Most of all, I believe that leveraging our presence in these social communities generates word of mouth, which in any form of business is the most valuable advertising. Every action I make online, specifically in the social sphere, for the business seeks as its end goal the generation of word-of-mouth.

> In my use of Facebook so far, I've begun building a strong initial following and to create a dialogue with our customer base leading up to our September hard opening. Twitter has been gaining in popularity among the foodies, which is awesome considering I set up the account only a week ago. We have a Klout score of 12! Woo woo! *I anticipate*

combining its power with Foursquare to help us to truly unlock our social growth as we roll around Philly. Having the ability to *tweet our next location instantly* to our followers for free saves us money and is convenient for the customer. Adding the thrill of checking into our location and receiving deals and *competing for mayorship (which brings with it larger deals)* provides a fresh and thrilling experience for the socially connected consumer.

Another interesting feature I've been playing around with is the concept of photo tagging. An on-truck digital camera will upload pictures of happy (consenting) customers directly to Facebook, encouraging them to tag themselves. In this sense, I am playing off the whole "cheese-steak-Polaroid's-on-the-wall-of-mom-and-pop" type experience without the clutter of physical photos. Consequently, with the exponential spread that Facebook's platform encourages, our brand will grow in a virally organic way.

Since it's ridiculous to rely on people's memories, I don't depend on them tagging themselves at home in our photos. *My solution, is that they can do it right off of our trucks' built-in iPads while they wait for their food."*

Okay, seriously, how brilliant is that last part? Get them when they're there. Have them tag right there! He's right—memory is fickle. Until we have people walking around with ginko biloba patches, I'm all for the food truck's idea: Get people when they first come in. Give them a reason not only to come back, but also to talk to you on the spot. Have them tag themselves on your iPad as they wait. What's an iPad cost now? $500 fully loaded? Where's the problem here? Spending $500 for continued brand loyalty for the next several years from hundreds if not thousands of people? Worthwhile investment, huh?

Case Study: Inclind, Inc.

How about another one?

Inclind, Inc. (@inclindinc) is a web development company founded in 1999 by Shaun Tyndall. What began as a one-man, home office venture quickly sprouted into a full-time business with 10 employees, a success built mostly on quality work and word of mouth. Unlike a lot of web development companies, Inclind, Inc., is located in Georgetown, Delaware, posing a unique marketing problem. How can a company in a relatively rural area market itself to companies in nearby cities like Washington, D.C., and Philadelphia?

Traditional methods such as Google ads were not working. They had to create interest, presence, and personality, not buy ad space.

They dusted off their Facebook account, a place where they can keep fans and friends up-to-date with news, site launches, and photos, putting some staff members in charge of updating and interacting with people. They also changed strategy for their Twitter account from focusing on *me me me* to *you you you* (where *you* is whomever they interact with). Taking proactive interest in industry-specific hashtags such as #drupal, #cms, #webdesign, #wordpress, and #php, they saw an increase in site traffic and Requests for Proposals from beyond their geographic region (new clients!).

A growing Twitter presence combined with an internal marketing strategy helped Inclind form partnerships, friendships, and contacts they would have never made otherwise. These relationships have led to website projects ranging from business start-ups, government entities, and celebrity websites; it has also broadened their people network. The simple things they did made them money.

Opportunities don't always come through a contact form. If people don't know you exist, you simply are not an option to them. Be social.

BE. SOCIAL.

We were taught to be social to begin with, right? We were "socialized" from nursery school on. So, why are we so afraid to be social now? For the first time, being social is actually required to make our professional careers stand out. So let's be social!

Case Study: Which Wich Superior Sandwiches

Here's another example, and this one is just super-awesome. Remember that social media tends to favor crisis. Whether that's good or bad, though, is up to you. Let's talk food—sandwiches, to be precise. How can you turn a sandwich into a hit on *The Tonight Show*?

Which Wich Superior Sandwiches is headquartered in Dallas, Texas. The sandwich chain is best known for its customized sandwiches, creative ordering system, and personalized sandwich bag. They offer more than 50 varieties of toasted sandwiches made with more than 40 quality meats, cheeses, vegetables, spreads, and sauces. They operate more than 100 franchise locations in 18 states. That's nice, but from a viral perspective? Yawn. Until late one night, their CEO, Jeff Sinelli, received an unusual email that his Cumming, Georgia, franchisee had forwarded from a customer. The email and accompanying emergency room photos explained that her husband and regular customer, Chad Ettmueller, had spent 14 hours in three different emergency rooms. His mouth had locked open after attempting to bite into a double meat version of the store's popular and aptly named "Wicked" sandwich. She had emailed to ask if he could possibly get a replacement sandwich.

In an age where photos can be retouched and pranks run rampant on the Internet, they all asked themselves: Is it real? If so, is the customer okay? And, uh, oh...are we going to get sued and have a PR crisis on our hands? At that point, Jeff reached out to Amy Power and her firm, Power Public Relations, to discuss how to navigate this strange territory. The two agreed late that night that Which Wich had a golden, one-time opportunity to leverage this unique storyline and create positive press and national awareness around a potentially negative situation. The key was discovering if the family would join in some potential fun or be the company's worst nightmare. After all, they had discovered that Chad had made a career out of structuring and brokering settlements.

Power Public Relations immediately recommended that Which Wich capture the story in a YouTube-style video. Jeff and their videographer flew to Atlanta that weekend to visit with Chad and interview him and even staged a funny reenactment of the story.

Additionally, Which Wich had to ramp up their social media accounts. They were open but were not being utilized to their full potential. The agency developed a quick online strategy to socialize the story, engage consumers, and promote various social media accounts by allowing consumers to vote on the sandwich's honorary name. Power Public Relations pitched a key restaurant trade writer via Facebook, breaking the news to the restaurant industry. It was picked up the following day by a *Los Angeles Times* food blogger and began to find its way onto other blogs. Meanwhile, the team finalized and loaded the YouTube videos, all within 48 hours.

The media relations team steadily pursued national media and garnered placements on AOL News, the Huffington Post, CNBC.com, the *Atlanta Journal and Constitution*, NPR, and others, adding more fuel to the story. These stories embedded the YouTube video and included information about the social media accounts and renaming contest, which sent the YouTube views skyrocketing and increased awareness for the Which Wich Twitter and Facebook accounts practically overnight.

The biggest highlight of the campaign for Which Wich was watching Jay Leno retell the story on *The Tonight Show*, ad-libbing and joking about the sandwich and America's new "hero." Within a few short months, the Which Wich Twitter account doubled its followers; the Facebook account went from 0 to nearly 1,000 fans; the YouTube channel received over 40,000 views; and the PR team delivered media placements valued at more than $500,000 in equivalent advertising spend—more than 15 times the return on their investment!

As for Chad, his jaw healed and he was able to tackle the sandwich that once had him beat. And recently, he was dining in his regular Which Wich restaurant when he overheard a young boy order the "Lockjaw."

Summary (and a Challenge)

I think you hear social media knocking, and I think you know it's coming in. Whatcha gonna do?

Any of these case studies can be easily applied to your company. They all have several key items in common:

1. The company realizes there is a need to communicate.

2. The company understands there's a way to not only disseminate information, but also to invite conversation and promote two-way dialogue.

3. The company attempts, in several ways, to integrate item two.

4. The company increases what works and decreases what doesn't.

When you think about it, that's not too hard.

I'll even make a deal with you: come up with an idea and then send me an email about it (peter@shankman.com). Let me take a look and see if I can't suggest any other ideas that might work.

Come on. Seriously. Email me. Or Twitter me: @petershankman. Or Facebook me: //facebook.com/petershankman. But don't email me with, "Hey, what social media idea should I implement?" That's boring.

Email me ideas that you think are awesome. I'll let you know what I think. When was the last time you got that from a book?

Go. Create. Email. You're welcome.

5

Social Media Damage Control: Stopping Small Problems from Becoming Big Ones

In this chapter, we'll take a look at how to handle small social media problems before they become big problems.

Special Chapter Guest: The PITA

So here's the funny thing. If you're reading this book in order, chances are you read the last paragraph in Chapter 4 and are thinking, "Woo-hoo! We know how to deal with the big problems! Bring 'em on!"

Which is true. You do. Except for one small thing. The big problems are rare. They'll still strike, and you need to know what to do with them, but chances are highly unlikely that the Big Problem is the one that's going to bring down your company.

Nope. Chances are, the small problems will get you first. They'll build up, grow in size, and take you down. You won't even realize it until your foundation is 85% chewed up. In the world of social media and customer service, the small problems hurt a lot more than the big problems.

The key then, obviously, is to handle the small problems before they become big problems. Is this a lot easier said than done? Well, kind of.

Big problems never start out as big problems. Like weeds, they start out small. The problem comes when you ignore them. Then they start to grow. Next thing you know, your lawn is destroyed.

Now instead of a lawn, what if it was your company?

I know what you're thinking. "It's one person! He has a complaint! How is he going to take down my company?" Well, 50 years ago, heck, 20 years ago, you would have been right.

Imagine the guy on the corner handing out leaflets explaining why no one should go into your store. He was wronged, and now he's going to tell the world. Problem is, he's handing out those leaflets to people who have already made the trip, found a spot to park, gotten out of the car, and walked toward the store. Chances are, he's not going to be that persuasive.

But, what if that same person, instead of waiting outside your store, was able to get to all of your customers before they left their houses? Not only that, but he was able to recommend a better place for them to go, and it was closer and cheaper and had nicer employees? Finally, what if his message got out there, not only to your customers, but your customers' friends, and their friends, and so on, and so on?

Makes you wish you'd been a tad nicer to your original complainer when he first had his problem, huh? That's what social media has become, and that's what it has done to your customer service. More importantly, that's what it can do to your business. It can ruin you if you're not careful.

But if you are careful, social media can vault your business to new heights, too. That's the part we're going to work on: How to avoid the bad by focusing on the good.

The end goal: Turn the complainer into a friend, turn the hater into a lover, and turn the video of your bad mistake into multiple videos about how great you are.

It's not hard. It takes a little bit of work, but it's no more difficult than any of the other advertising and marketing you're doing on a regular basis. The difference is that the payoff can be SO much more massive here, if done right.

So let's do it right.

First Things First: Different Types of Complainers

The first thing you need to recognize is that social media gives everyone a platform and gives them that platform with total and complete ease. Back in the day, as I mentioned earlier, it was all about the letter to the editor, the reporter who might have covered your problem, or your writing to "News 7 On Your Side" and hoping you got lucky. Maybe, in extreme cases, it was the Better Business Bureau or the attorney general. Most often, though, it was just you complaining and one or two people hearing your cries.

And the company was in control.

The Internet changed that. We have instant voices now. Just add connectivity. Not happy? Blast it out on Twitter. Feel like you got wronged? Post about it on Facebook. Didn't get the right thing, whatever that may be? Go online to the company's blog or fan page and go to town. Are you wronged and just a bit tech savvy? Make a video. See "United Breaks Guitars" on YouTube, with close to 9,000,000 views (http://www.youtube.com/watch?v=5YGc4zOqozo).

Welcome to the world of social media. Complaining has never been easier.

It doesn't matter if you run a multibillion dollar airline or a small mom-and-pop gas station. Anyone can complain about you if they feel wronged, and it's easy to get it online where the world can see it. Don't believe me? Go to Google and search for "bad customer service." When I did that (see http://3.ly/bKEw), I found more than 145 million results. Try it yourself. Go have fun.

Where does that leave us? Well, social media can make anyone a complainer. It allows anyone with a computer or Internet-connected device (and let's face it, even the cheapest cell phone nowadays is still an Internet-connected device) to broadcast what you did wrong and how upset they are with you in pretty close to real time.

But to fix the problems, or even work the problem to find the solution, you need to identify the types of complainers. They are as follows:

- **The never-complained-before complainer**—This is someone to whom you should react immediately. This person has never complained about your service before. In fact, you've never even heard of him. You have to take action immediately because you don't know whether this person is really angry or if he's really the "multi-complainer" as described next. But either way, if this person is a new complainer and you don't know him, you need to react. The most common complaint is that something has really screwed up and he wasn't expecting it, probably because he has had good service in the past.

- **The multi-complainer complainer**—This person is a pain. This person likes to hear himself talk and, lucky you, your company happens to now be in his crosshairs. Search his history and you'll see that virtually everything he says is a complaint, a downer, and he's the one no one wants to hang out with at parties. You need to offer a placation to him, but do it quickly, make it something easy, and get him off your radar. Chances are that he won't be happy with any solution you give him, so your best bet is to just get him handled and gone. His most frequent complaint is whatever happens to be the sand in his shoe today.

- **The I-can't-believe-he's-complaining-he's-our-most-frequent-customer-who-always-said-nice-things-about-us-in-the-past complainer**—Danger, Will Robinson! Danger! This is your most deadly complainer, and whatever you're working on should be dropped immediately to handle this person. Remember the old adage that 10% of our customers bring in 90% of our revenue? Well, this is one of those 10%.

Most likely something really stupid got him really mad, and now you need to react. This isn't the time for ignoring. His most frequent complaint is that he rarely complains; he usually compliments. So that means something is really up. Get your hustle on!

- **The one-with-photos-and-videos-and-multiple-camera-angles complainer**—Another toughie, this one has the tools and isn't afraid to use them. He probably knows his tech, too. He's uploading photos and videos of the problem as it happens in real time because that's what he's good at. The quicker you respond, even if it's not a full-fledged solution right away, the better chance you'll have at getting him to cease-fire to see what you come up with. Then, of course, you have to come up with something. His most frequent complaint is anything that makes for good video or still photos.

- **The Dear @cnnbreakingnews complainer**—This is the one who believes that any wrong he has suffered deserves the attention of mass media, and he'll be sure to cc all the Twitter and Facebook accounts he can find at any given time, each time. Fortunately, he's the first cousin of the multi-complainer, so you can tend to handle him quickly and forget it. His most frequent complaint is anything that ends with "And you should totally do a story on this."

So how do you handle them? First, let's take a look at things you should do when you receive any complaint.

Overarching Rules for Handling any Complaint

The moment you see a complaint, do the following:

1. Record the time of the first complaint. Not when you saw it, but when it was posted.

2. Check your files (you have files, right?) and see whether the person's name comes up in any type of customer record. Examples might be:

   - VIP?

   - Multiuser?

   - Problem customer?

3. If the customer doesn't show up in any of the files, start a new record for her. Record the following:

   - Name

   - Time of complaint

- Nature of complaint

4. Check to see a level of popularity, based on the kind of complaint:

- Public complaint: (Posted somewhere)

Facebook:

- How many friends does she have?

- Are comments coming in?

Twitter

- How many followers does she have?

- Is she being retweeted? Check http://search.twitter.com and take three words from her original tweet, such as "flight from EWR" and see whether other retweets are coming up.

Blog post

- Her blog?

Check http://alexa.com for a ranking – Is her blog popular?

Check to see what other kinds of posts she has written: Do they go back a ways? Are most of them complaints?

Search her blog to see if there are any other mentions of your company name. If so, are they positive? Negative?

- Your blog (Comments)

When was the commenter account created?

Has she commented under the same name before? If so, were the comments positive? Negative?

- A third-party post (Yelp, TripAdvisor, and so on)

Has she posted before?

Has she posted before about you?

Handling Different Kinds of Complainers

Now, let's look at a sample complaint or two from each complainer and discuss the best ways to deal with each.

You might need to take several steps to handle some complainers, while others can be handled by just taking one action. And, obviously, the suggestions here are intended to be broad in scope. Each complainer will be just a little bit different. The goal is not only to fix the problem and turn the complainer into a fan, but also to learn from what the complainer is complaining about and prevent it from happening in the future. Do both, and that truly counts as a social media win.

The Never-Complained-Before Complainer

Imagine sitting down at a restaurant and as you're about to order, someone passes your table and says, "Oh, don't order that; it's terrible," and keeps walking. You'd have no idea where he came from or why you should trust this random person. With the exception of a very peeved waiter, most likely nothing would change and you'd continue to order your meal. Life would go on, and you'd shake your head at the crazy man who told you not to order.

Now, let's try it again. Instead of the random crazy guy showing up as you're ordering, what if you were reading a review of the same restaurant the day before you went there. The review would go something like this:

> Fred206: I used to come to Joe's Pub at least once a week. The food was superb, the wait staff was kind and fun, and the atmosphere was spectacular. Loved this place. Then, they got new management. Within six months, the portion sizes went down, the food quality went to hell, and the majority of the original wait staff quit. The last time I went there, it was a ghost town, my food was terrible, and it was just pretty depressing. As someone who used to eat here regularly, it's really sad. I can't recommend this place anymore. Go somewhere else."

That review would stick with you. Why? It's factual. It's full of specifics, bullet points, and case-by-case reasons why you shouldn't eat there. It's not the random crazy man shouting from the rooftops, but rather, specific reasons why you shouldn't eat at that restaurant.

That's what you're up against when you get alerted to that first negative review or comment and you don't know who this person is or where he's from. He's out of the blue, yet he posts a scathing review or comment, full of specific facts. You need to act:

1. **Reach Out.** This will most likely be step one in every kind of complaint. You want to make initial contact, and you want to do it fast. Initial contact will accomplish many things. First and foremost, it'll staunch the bleeding. When a medic reaches the scene of a car accident, her job is to get the victim as stable as possible as quickly as possible, while transporting the victim to a place where better help can be obtained. Your initial job is to be that medic. Reaching out usually accomplishes this right off the bat. The complainer stops whatever he is

doing, just for a second, to see what you're going to do—much like a cat who looks up from whatever it's doing the second you run the can opener.

2. **Listen.** Once you've reached out, you've made initial contact. You've put the ball in the complainer's court. One of two things can happen at this point:

- The complainer will contact you as you requested.

- She won't even notice you attempted to make contact, and the situation will go away.

As far as you're concerned, both of these outcomes are favorable to you. The key to resolving the situation, though, is the follow-up. I suggest reaching out for that initial contact in a very simple way:

"Joan3482: My name is Peter, and I work with Company XYZ. We'd love to talk to you personally about the comments you left and see how we can make your specific situation right, as well as use this as a way to improve our service overall. I would appreciate it if you could contact me directly. My email is xyz@xyzcorp.com."

You can modify this response to be outlet specific. The previous response would obviously work on a blog or Facebook. Twitter needs to be shorter. For example:

"Joan3482: I'm Peter, and I work with Company XYZ. Please email me at xyz@xyzcorp.com so we can fix this and make it right."

 Tip

Have a secondary email address that looks like your first email address but isn't. So if your first email address is **peter@shankman.com**, make your backup email address **peter.shankman@shankman.com**. What you're doing is providing a definite way to contact you, but even if your email is shared (which it will be), it won't bog you down during your regular day of work. (You still have to check the email, though. Don't forget about it!)

Two things can happen here. Joan will email you, or Joan won't email you. Either way, you've shown that you're listening and more than willing to respond immediately to complaints to fix the problem.

Assuming she does email you, listen first. Ask her what happened. Work with her to find a solution. Then, when everyone is happy, post to the same place from where the conversation started. Thank her for working with you and remaining a customer. This puts the conversation to bed. Life goes on; everyone's happy.

The Multi-Complainer Complainer

Everyone knows this guy. Most times, you go out of your way to avoid him. You'd rather walk face first into the bowl of Ranch dip at the party then have him catch your eye and engage you in conversation. Why? Because he's always complaining. You can't escape him. Whether he's complaining about the weather or the service he received at his local pancake place, it's rare he has a happy word to share.

Here's the interesting thing about the multi-complainer, though. Because all he does is complain, he's not only the least popular person at the salad bar, but also the least credible. This is huge for you because his lack of credibility means he also lacks true power to seriously damage you.

Knowing this, there are several ways to respond to the multi-complainer. I prefer to choose the path of least resistance, though. For example, let's say Mr. Multi-Complainer posts the following complaint:

> " I went to dinner at Joe's Diner last night and I was truly disappointed – Bread was totally hard, and they only gave me one free basket. #FAIL."

Here's how I recommend that you handle this kind of complaint:

1. **Back up and read prior tweets or posts.** Chances are you'll find a variety of complaints reading something like this:

> " I had breakfast last week at Bob's Breakfast joint, and the eggs were runny. I demand compensation. #FAIL"

> " Flew from EWR to LAX last week, and my flight was 30 minutes delayed, and I had a middle seat. Never flying JoeAirlines Again. #FAIL"

> " Brought my car to Joe's House of Oil Change, and they gave me a car air freshener that was totally not fresh. Never going back again. #FAIL"

> By this point, not only are you seeing a pattern, but trust me, all of his followers are as well. And based on that, his followers are probably quite limited. So limit your response. Respond, but do so in a way that shuts down the situation:

> "Hey @multicomplainer – Sorry to hear your bread wasn't fresh during your last visit to Joe's Diner. Show this tweet on your mobile device next time you eat at Joe's, and we'll comp you a free dessert to make up for it."

> Or, if you're feeling a little more generous, make it worth it for him and a few friends by offering free drinks to the group. This promotes the

concept of sharing, which is one of the key tenets of social media. If he has the ability to share his good fortune, he will—in every media outlet possible to him. It makes him cooler, and because he can't be cool in this instance while still complaining about you, one of the two will have to go away. You can bet complaining about you will lose out to looking cool every time. Here's a sample response:

"Hey @multicomplainer – Sorry to hear your bread wasn't fresh during your last visit to Joe's – Let us know the next time you want to come in, and we'll buy you and three friends a round of drinks on Joe."

Now, you've just earned good karma, not only from your old nemesis @multicomplainer (who's now a friend), but also all of his friends. Well done. Situation resolved. Much like a small child who falls down and only cries if he notices that someone is paying attention, the multi-complainer just wants to be heard and recognized. Do that, in the simplest form, and you'll turn the multi-complainer into a multi-fan. And, hey, that's one of the purest goals of social media.

Here's one final thought on the multi-complainer. It's always a good lesson to go and read the rest of the multi-complainer's Twitter stream or Facebook page. It's a great way to learn what other problems he's having with other companies and a way for you to figure out how to avoid them in the future with future customers.

The I-Can't-Believe-He's-Complaining Complainer

This is the one complainer I hope you rarely get. This is the complainer who can, without question, cause the most trouble for you and your business. He's the one who can take you down for several reasons:

1. He's a loyal user/member/fan/flyer/buyer. Whatever he is, he's loyal. So if he's wronged, it's not just by "some company." It's personal.

2. Loyal users tend to be more connected, have bigger audiences, and rarely complain. The whole reason they're loyal in the first place is because they get great service. If you get great service, you're likely to spend a lot of money with the company. It's a revolving cycle. So when something goes wrong and the complaint happens, the world hears it.

3. From a strictly financial point of view, when one of your most frequent customers who usually says nice things about you has a problem, your whole company has a much bigger problem. Among other things, consider this a big, big warning sign.

Here's a good example of a situation I had recently with Continental Airlines—what happened, how the story broke, where it went, and how it was resolved.

I fly Continental Airlines a few hundred thousand miles per year, easily. I'm one of those 10% of their flyers that brings in 90% of their revenue. You know how that goes.

I usually compliment them. "Thanks Continental, for the upgrade!" or something similar. That kind of response is quite normal for me, and based on how much I travel, I'm definitely one of the most positive voices for Continental Airlines.

Let's think about that for a second. I'm actively engaged in the art of complimenting a company with whom I spend a ridiculous amount of money every month. Why would I do that?

The answer is quite simple: brand loyalty. I love Continental because I've established a relationship with them. Everyone knows I fly Continental. I'm the mayor on FourSquare (http://foursquare.com/users/shankman) of several routes and airline clubs within the network and frequently recommend Continental to friends and colleagues as my airline of choice. So obviously, if I'm upset, it's something worth taking notice of.

I should also mention I rarely check baggage. I've spent two weeks on another continent with only carry-on luggage. I won't date someone who checks luggage. (Okay, that might be a bit of an exaggeration, but you get the idea.)

So when I had to check luggage for a flight to Texas, you can imagine my shock when I landed, went to baggage claim, and waited for my luggage. And waited, and waited. I waited longer than people in Casablanca waited to get to America.

And nothing.

After asking the baggage claim person at the very, very small airport and receiving an "I dunno, fill out this form," I sent out a tweet (see Figure 5.1).

Figure 5.1   *I tweeted this after Continental lost my luggage.*

Notice that five people retweeted it immediately. Of course, the bigger issue was that more than 100 people commented, rewrote it, or reposted it on Twitter alone.

I also posted something similar on Facebook (see Figure 5.2).

Figure 5.2   *I was able to include more detail in my Facebook post.*

Note the 99 comments.

This was a Friday night, around 6:45 p.m. Eastern time. Chances are, you wouldn't expect many people to be around at Continental to answer, let alone care. And on many airlines, you might be right.

Continental, however, recognized the issue. Within an hour, I received a call on my mobile phone from the head of baggage services at Continental, first letting me know that my bag had been found, then letting me know that it was on the next flight, and finally apologizing for the problem I had.

Let's analyze Continental's response. They didn't apologize first. Instead, they started the conversation by immediately telling me what the resolution to my specific problem was, how it would be resolved, how long it would take, and when all would be right. Only when they confirmed that I understood that my issue was resolved, did they offer an apology.

And that's the right thing to do.

It's important to understand that when you have a problem, your never-complained-before customer doesn't care that you're sorry. Your customer doesn't want to hear, "We understand you're upset." All your customer wants to hear is that you're fixing the problem and the resolution will occur at X time, and at Y place, resulting is Z satisfaction.

Anything else is window dressing. Fix the problem; then apologize. Continental did that.

So what was the end result for me, the customer who never complains? I got my bag after a little more than a two-hour wait. Continental kept a customer, and more importantly, I immediately went back to my complimenting-the-company-I-spend-a-fortune-with ways (see Figure 5.3).

Figure 5.3 *And Mr. Never-Complained-Before Customer is back to his old self.*

So, here's a quick rule review on how to handle the customer-who-never-com-plains-and-is-all-of-a-sudden-complaining:

1. When you see the complaint, it's go-time. This isn't a customer who is used to waiting around, especially not from the company he really likes. Get on it immediately.

2. Fix the problem, or at least come up with a temporary solution that's worthwhile.

3. Get in touch with the customer immediately.

4. Save the apologies for last. Explain first how you're fixing the problem and what the resolution will be. The apologies come afterward.

5. Follow up as many times as it takes.

I've worked with some companies to create a best-customer list. The second a complaint is noticed from any customer, this best-customer list is cross-checked, and if the complainer is on it, the rules listed previously are instituted. If not, they go back to the checklist for the never-complained-before complainer.

To paraphrase *Animal Farm*—All customers matter. But on occasion, some matter a little more than others.

The One-with-Photos-and-Videos-and-Multiple-Camera-Angles Complainer

This is a fun complainer, and if you play your cards right, you can turn her into a fan for life, complete with her own multimedia library!

Think about everyone you know. Now think about their mobile phones. Do you know one person with a mobile phone without a camera in it? Probably not.

Let's face it. We're a society of citizen journalists, recording and documenting everything we see and uploading it to the world in the hopes that they'll find it as interesting as we do.

This is beneficial when you find yourself sitting next to a celebrity on an airplane or when your cat happens to learn how to do a back-flip, but not so beneficial when you run a company and something goes majorly wrong. In fact, the video evidence is there for you to choke on and the rest of the world to gawk on. So, the question becomes not how to avoid people taking pictures, but how to react when they do.

Because they will.

You're going to become aware of the multimedia complainer the same way you become aware of the others—Google alerts, Twitter updates, the usual. The problem is that they'll usually come with a link attached. That's the dead giveaway that there's more to the picture than just a complainer. The link is your sign that there's more to come, and you'd better be prepped.

Multimedia can come in any form: audio, photos, or even (heaven forbid) video. But they all have the potential to bring you down.

So let's look at Figure 5.4, which was snapped as someone was walking onto an airplane.

In Figure 5.4 you can see toward the back of the plane, a baggage handler sleeping on the baggage loading ramp.

Sleeping.

This was tweeted out with a note reading, "SERIOUSLY, (AIRLINE NAME) – Are You KIDDING ME?"

Within minutes, the photo was retweeted a few dozen times; then it got bigger, and bigger, and by the time that flight landed, the photo had been seen by thousands of people.

How do you stop this from happening?

Well, the simple fact is, you can't. While there are probably hundreds of rules the baggage loaders have to learn, I doubt there's one that blatantly reads "don't sleep on the baggage loader."

Figure 5.4   *Photo of sleeping airline employee, posted via a mobile device (BlackBerry) through UberTwitter (www.ubertwitter.com) and retweeted hundreds of times in seconds.*

What you can do, though, is get in front of the situation. Drop an @reply to the person who originally broke the story on Twitter.

To find the original tweet on Twitter (before hundreds of retweets), take several words from the tweet—but not the whole tweet. Put it in quotes, and Google it. Your search would look something like this: "AIRLINE NAME) –"SERIOUSLY, (AIRLINE NAME)."

Putting your search in quotes avoids false positives. Then all you have to do is simply scroll backward to the earliest mention of the phrase. Chances are, that's the person who broke your story.

Once you have that, a simple tweet suffices:
"@multimediacomplainer – Thank you for bringing this to our attention. We'll be investigating this matter and getting back to you ASAP."

Notice that you didn't offer to fix the problem. It technically wasn't the original poster's problem. It's not like you're going to prevent her from making her flight because there's a baggage handler sleeping on her plane.

 Tip

Always react to the problem by first identifying what type of problem it is. Apologizing for the sleeping baggage handler won't help you. No one was "wronged," per se. But it is a blight on your company, and one that should be fixed. So fix it, announce that you're fixing it, and then move on.

Nothing you can do here will right anyone's personal wrong, simply because there was no personal wrong. Someone snapped a photo she thought was funny or frustrating and posted it. There's nothing you can do, per se. You got nailed. Deal with it and move on. Think of it this way, too—if the story gets posted and goes away, there's no reason to communicate it any further than to issue the thank you I suggested. If it does gain some legs, then you have the good reply and apology already, and you can move on.

I'd also add, work with your team to make your own baggage handler understand why he shouldn't sleep on the loading ramp. Just adjust to your own situation.

Dealing with Complaints That *Are* Personal

What if the complaint is personal to someone?

Let's take a look at what I call the "My Stay at the Hotel Ghetto Episode" and the resulting follow-up.

Here's the short version: Someone stays at a hotel chain that usually provides incredibly good service, except this particular hotel does the exact opposite, with broken items and holes in the wall. Said someone has a camera with him and writes a blog post. Results follow.

What would you do if you came in one morning and found a blog post comparing staying at your hotel to sleeping in the fictional Quik-E-Mart made popular by the TV show *The Simpsons*? Most probably, you'd have a bad day. Well, take a look at Figure 5.5.

Turns out, one of your properties in Florida was very rude to a man with several cameras. Additionally, he was put in a room that not only had exposed wiring from holes cut in the wall, but also had a shower that broke—in mid-shower (see Figure 5.6).

If you were the hotel-chain parent, you'd be having a super bad day, especially if you were being compared to a fictional deli famous for month-old milk.

So, what do you do to fix the problem?

If you're this particular brand, you get on the phone almost immediately with the customer having the problem and you explain that there was absolutely no excuse for the service the customer received, the state of the hotel, or the fact that things were broken. Then, you let the customer know that you're going into discussions with the CEO of the chain and will report back in 24 hours.

Then you do it.

Figure 5.5 *Yup. Those are exposed wires. In your hotel room. And, currently, up on the Internet, thanks to a blog post.*

Figure 5.6 *Adding insult to injury, the shower broke on this unlucky traveler.*

That's what this hotel brand did, and the next day, they called the guest back not only with a complete refund, but also with a whole bunch of loyalty points for his mileage account and a famous dual-showerhead made popular by the hotel in question.

And what did the wronged guest do? He wrote a follow-up blog post explaining the situation and the fix. The guest was happy and wanted to share it. The brand was happy because they fixed the guest's problem and made the guest happy again. The specific hotel in question? Well, they got a pretty good talking to, no doubt.

It seems so incredibly simple, doesn't it? Well, it is and it isn't.

The simple part:

1. Listen.

2. React.

3. Make it right.

The not-so-simple part:

1. Finding the customer to whom the problem belongs.

2. Finding out if it was as bad as the images make it out to be.

3. If it was, finding out what you can do to fix it.

4. Getting in touch with the customer to let him know you're fixing it.

5. Actually fixing it.

Piece of cake, right?

We've already discussed the simple part. That's easy. You should already be listening, and you should know what to do when your listening hooks in a complainer with multimedia.

Now you need to focus on how to make the multimedia complainer happy.

If the complainer is already using multimedia, he is probably a technophile. Technophiles like technology—they keep it with them most of the time and they love to play with it. How can you use that to your advantage?

Everyone likes to feel as if they're making a difference. Explaining to the complainer that his information, video, audio, or images are going to help fundamentally improve the company is one way. This, of course, is after you've made the complainer happy.

For our hotel complainer in the previous example, it was about listening and reacting based on a specific problem. Because the shower broke while the complainer was in it—and this was mentioned in the blog—the complainer was sent a very expensive showerhead.

This showed that the hotel chain listened, but it also showed that they cared enough to make sure the customer was satisfied with the resolution to the **specific** problem he had. It's not like just offering a gift card.

The chain listened and responded with an appropriate gift. It was also an expensive gift that's not usually seen outside of hotels. What does this mean for the multimedia complainer? It's a chance to show off the new gift, via photos and video. And, of course, because photos are useless without explanation, it's yet another chance for the complainer to turn his complaint into a compliment and show the beautiful showerhead—that is, the expensive gift.

Look at that, The hotel chain is now a chain that has great taste and goes out of its way to make its customers happy.

What can you do to make the multimedia complainer happy?

- Can you offer him another chance to stay/buy/eat and have him bring his camera again?

- Can you send him video of the improvements you've made to your location/property/product/food so he can use it in a follow-up post on his blog?

- Can you offer him a way to come back/eat again/try a new version and do a live video of the arrival/unwrap/eat?

- Can you offer him an unboxing? These are huge. Whenever we have a client send a new product to a blogger, we box the product just like it would be in the store. Bloggers love unboxing photos, from the initial opening to taking the item out. It's almost like a time capsule. What can you do to offer your multimedia complainer the chance to do that?

You want the multimedia complainer to use his powers for good, not evil. Make that your mission. Once you get him on your side, he'll be an amazingly powerful force for you!

Imagine—once he's on your side, what if you tried the following?

"Hey Mike (because now he's a friend and not a complainer anymore) – We've got a launch party on Saturday for the new version of that thing you love. Want to come and take some photos and videos, and we'll give you VIP access?"

Or how about:

> "Hey Mike – Peter here from the Hotel You Had A Problem With
> Before We Fixed It" – We're launching our new upgraded suites hotel –
> Let me know the next time you're in town – We'll upgrade you to a
> suite – on us!"

Not only is this great because you know he'll blog/photo/video/audio it, but it's also great follow-up! And that's something of which you can never, ever do enough.

The @cnnbreakingnews Complainer

Finally, we come to the @cnnbreakingnews complainer.

This is easy. The @cnnbreakingnews complainer simply assumes that everything that happens to her is horrible and worthy of national attention. In fact, there's nothing worse going on in the world—no wars, no famines, no natural disasters— that could possibly be as bad as our complainer having to sleep on a lumpy pillow in a hotel, or not getting the right latte, or (gasp!) getting an order in the mail that's broken!

It's the social media equivalent of shouting, "Don't you know who I am?!" to the maitre 'd who won't seat you. It rarely works.

If it's your first time seeing it, though, it can freak you out. But stop for a second, take a deep breath, and think.

What's @cnnbreakingnews complainer mad about? What happened to her? It's probably not something that's going to light up news bureaus from Boston to Baghdad.

Unless she has video of the CEO saying, "We're never going to serve her, and we're going to kill her family, too," or video of a product of yours exploding in flames and engulfing a basket full of puppies, the media probably won't care.

So, while you don't have to go into massive crisis mode, that doesn't mean you should ignore the @cnnbreakingnews complainer. Quite the opposite—you can calm her down and turn her into a fan, so that if the time comes when the media actually does pay attention to one of her rants, you'll be on her "nice" list.

What's the best way to do this? As previously described with every other type of complainer, a simple note is a good start, followed by a follow-up note after you get a response.

The big thing to remember about the @cnnbreakingnews complainer is that she likes to hear herself talk. She does this every time she feels wronged, so there are probably already a bunch of complaint emails out there. (See the section titled, "The Multi-Complainer Complainer," earlier in this chapter.)

You can get through it by realizing that it's never a slow enough news day to give credence to someone whose soup was cold when it was supposed to be hot. Be nice and apologize, and you should move on without too much grief.

Wrap-up

For as many complaints as there are out there, there are just as many complainers. Your job is using the tools in your social media arsenal to identify them, figure out what type of complainer they are, figure out how to handle them, and do so with the least blowback to your company or brand.

It comes down to good recordkeeping, good analysis, and (of course) good customer service.

One thing we tell our clients is that you shouldn't think of the complainers as a group you have to satisfy, but rather, as a unique opportunity to turn a regular customer into a raving fan who can do your PR for you. He is obviously familiar with the broadcast tools necessary to get his word out. If you're smart enough to fix his problem before it becomes a problem or, even better, make him super-happy after he has a problem, you can turn this avid broadcaster into a fan who does your PR for you and tells the world how great you are because of how great you made him feel.

And that...well, that's just good social customer service.

Making Customer Addicts Online: Best Practices That Work!

"You'll be fine, as long as you don't do anything stupid."

One of my favorite jokes was told to me by a professor I had at Boston University. He told me about the difference between advertising and PR.

He told me that advertising is when you're in a pub and see a beautiful woman across the bar from you. You walk up to her, tell her you're amazing, and expect her to come home with you. Chances are, you'll get a drink thrown in your face, as she rolls her eyes and turns back to her friends to talk about the idiot who just unsuccessfully tried to hit on her. That's advertising.

PR, on the other hand, is the opposite. PR is when I'm sitting at a bar minding my own business and two women on the other side of the bar are talking amongst themselves. One of them notices me, recognizes me, and spends five minutes telling her friend how amazing I am, what an awesome person I am, and how lucky she'd be to get to know me. Her friend then walks over and introduces herself to me. I go home with her. That, my friends, is great PR!

Here's the updated joke, including social media, with apologies to my journalism professor:

You start a Facebook fan page and then email everyone you've ever known, with suggestions that they "like" your group, whether it's relevant to them or not. The only thing all of these people have in common are air—as in, they're breathing it. You then bombard them with updates, emails, and invitations to events they'll never attend, all while hearing nothing but crickets as you see absolutely no action whatsoever from your page. That's advertising.

But, imagine if you went out of your way to actively engage every customer and potential customer who has ever bought or considered buying from you. Imagine if you spent a few minutes a day going over your message boards, emails, and Twitter mentions, personally responding not only to the haters, but to the fans, as well. Imagine you followed up with your buyers, customers, and clients, offering them a return discount if they posted a photo of themselves using your product on your fan page or sent you a quick video showing them outside one of your establishments.

Imagine if you emailed them to just say hi and ask how life was going with their new product. Or just to ask if they have any further thoughts now that their experience *with you is over. Now imagine them telling their friends, sending their colleagues to your website, and leaving comments on your blog. Imagine them recommending you to their friends. That, my friends, is* the new great PR.

Let's talk about how we can get us some of that!

A Few Rules of the Road

Here are some basic rules before we get started:

1. The customer is still always right (except on two occasions):

    *   **Occasion 1**—When you've done everything that could possibly be expected of you and the customer is still complaining

    *   **Occasion 2**—When the customer is mean to your staff

> ✉ *Note*
>
> Saying the customer is always right except when he is mean to your staff is a caveat that you can choose to use or not use. But think about this: In the end, good customer service has to come from the company as a whole. It comes from the company when the company feels good as a whole. If the company isn't feeling good, isn't feeling supported, customer service can't thrive. Remember that if you're afraid to give your employees access to social media on the company's behalf, that's not a social media problem— that's a *company* problem.

2. Don't wait for the customer to have a disagreement with you before you implement rule 1. The customer should be right from the second he walks in the door, and that feeling of rightness should permeate from the second he enters your establishment, logs on to your website, or calls your phone number. Here are two things to remember:

    *   A customer who feels at home and safe in an environment (especially an online environment) is more likely to make a purchase.

    *   A customer who *has* felt that way and is rewarded with the knowledge that his decision to purchase was the right one will tell other people about it. Not simply because he wants

to help you, but because he's essentially getting a small chance to brag about his decision-making process, whether he knows he is or not.

3. One happy customer with a reason to tell friends he's happy is worth five ads in a national newspaper.

4. Two happy customers starts an army.

So, How Do You Do It?

The Eastern philosopher Sun Tzu said it best—All battles are won long before they're ever fought on the battlefield.

The key to good customer service through social media starts in the company as a whole. If the company is happy, good customer service becomes second nature. Ever walk into a chain store and receive horrible customer service? The next time you do, take a moment to look around. Do you see any employees smiling? Do you see anyone working there who actually looks like they want to be there?

But, the next time you receive awesome customer service, note the same thing. See the smiles? See how the employees actually seem like they want to work there?

There's a reason so many companies strive to be on that famous magazine's "best places to work" list. The happier employees are, the better they'll be at administering stellar customer service.

From a social media point of view, it works the same way. Do you allow your employees to use social media? Do you put unnecessary restrictions on it?

Remember the old story about the kid who was allowed to curse growing up versus the kid who wasn't? The kid who was allowed to curse quickly realized that it was nothing more than words, and the concept of cursing quickly lost its appeal. Can you do that with social media? Not make it lose its appeal but, rather, lose its restrictions.

If you're able to trust your employees and let them use social media to help grow your company, they'll actually want to do it. If you have happy employees, give them the right to brag about that! How many employees do you know who actually brag about how awesome their jobs are?

Make their workplace awesome, and let them go online to talk about it. Recently, I was writing a huge social media guidebook for a massive insurance company. Their biggest fear? Not that people would comment on their Facebook page. Not that a Twitter account could open them up to lawsuits. Not even that someone would leave something negative in the comments. Their biggest fear was that an employee, if given the ability to use social media, would write something negative about the company.

I looked at the director of marketing and asked, "So, unless you give them access to social media in the workplace, they'll never use it? Not at their desks, not at home, not in their cars, and not on their mobile phones?"

It's not about restricting employees. It's about trusting them. Once you do that, you have the ability to open up social media to your customers and clients. But only then.

Trust your employees and explain that, while you trust them, they also need to be smart. Or as we say in the skydiving world, "You'll be fine, as long as you don't do anything stupid."

Let's look at two scenarios: the walk-in sequence and the online sequence. Both have a common, twofold goal—to get the customer to purchase something and to offer an experience so unmatched that the customer uses the tools at his disposal to tell others to do the same.

Tip

The goal of purchasing something should always be at the forefront, equally matched with customer service. Remember, social media for the sake of social media is pointless. Social media to increase sales and generate revenue is beneficial—not only for the company's bottom line, but also for your job. If you can't show the powers-that-be that there's money to be made (or even saved) with social media, the powers-that-be aren't going to care how cool the tools you get to use are. More than likely, they will be apt to restrict your access to the playground with all those cool tools.

So You Have a Physical Presence

Let's assume you're a store. It could be any type of store, from a record shop (remember them?) to an antiques store, to a local convenience mart. A new customer walks in, who you've never seen before. She buys—let's say it's a convenience store—a bottle of water and pack of gum. She pays for it and walks out. To her, that's no different from any other transaction at any other convenience store.

But, what if you work with your employees to make what I call "social small talk?" These are simple questions to ask while ringing up that water and gum. It could be as easy as this:

"One bottle of water, one stick of gum – $3.52. Nice BlackBerry. That the 9100?"

or

> "One bottle of water, one stick of gum - $3.52. Where'd you get that cool iPhone cover?"

You're bringing the customer into engagement. And it's not BS, unrelated engagement. You're asking her something that's personal to her. Never underestimate the close, personal relationship between a person and her mobile communications device. (Amazing to think that 20 years ago, none of us had them, huh?)

One of two types of responses will follow.

> "Yeah, that's the 9100. I just got it!" or "Yeah, I got the case at (wherever.)"

or

> "Huh? Yeah. Thanks for the gum."

If it's number two, okay, good effort. Try for the next customer. But if it's number one, start some follow-up:

> "Are you on Facebook?" (With more than 500 million members, chances are she is.)

"No."
"Okay, no worries. We have some promotions if you are."
"Yes."

> "Cool. You should like us at http://facebook.com/storename. The next time you come in for some gum, show us you're a fan and we'll give you a free (whatever)."

That's the most basic of them all. Facebook is today what email was in the late '90s—something everyone was doing. And even as it becomes more basic to our very existence, it is still somewhat of a novelty to the masses, enough so that a simple discount might be enough to get people interested on a most basic level.

 Tip

If you haven't already claimed your company fan page name on Facebook, start here: http://www.facebook.com/help/?page=904#!/pages/create.php

Inviting someone to "like" your company on Facebook is similar to asking someone out on a first date. You'd like her to get to know you better to form a mutually beneficial relationship. You're offering her something of value to do it, and she's doing the same—you offer her discounts and specials, and she offers you loyalty.

Of course, the mistake most people make is ending it here. They either join Facebook, or they don't. It doesn't matter to most companies either way because they tend to leave it at that. It's like that first date saying, "Yes, I'd love to go out with you," and then you not calling. Duh.

Every few days, take a look at your fan page and note your new users. Thank them. Drop them a quick FB mail and say thanks for joining, or post a status message thanking them publicly. Whatever you do, somehow acknowledge them. If you don't, there's no point in getting them to join in the first place.

Let's flip it. As the person comes up to pay, say she's texting furiously. Ask if she's on Twitter. If she says yes, invite her to follow you as well, and tell her you'll give her something if she does it on the spot.

Tip

Keep a reward jar at the checkout. This doesn't have to be anything expensive. It could be pens with your company logo on them, baseball caps, or branded bottle openers. Anything you can offer your customers for joining and showing their loyalty on the spot.

If the customer joins you on Twitter, note the time. Twitter sends you a note every time someone follows you. You can then track her and thank her more personally when the time comes.

Once you have her in any capacity (Twitter, Facebook, and so on), it's easy to get her in other places. Check out what Kum & Go, a convenience store chain of 450 stores in the Midwest, does on its Twitter page (see Figure 6.1).

Figure 6.1   *Kum & Go offers the ability to connect with its customers in several ways.*

See how they thank people for connecting with them and also offer them the option of connecting on Facebook and their blog as well? A multiconnected customer greatly increases her loyalty.

What can you do to do the same?

 Tip

Make sure that for as many points of contact you have, there are just as many ways for people to find those other points, no matter how they first find you.

So, you have them—either on Twitter or on Facebook. Now what? Remember this acronym—WARS:

- Make them feel **welcome**.

- Make them feel **appreciated**.

- Make them want to **return**.

- Make them want to **share**.

Follow the WARS acronym. You want to do the four items shown here with every customer or potential customer with whom you interact online. Why? Because if you do that, the one thing you DON'T have to do as much is PR because your customers will do it for you. (Remember my journalism professor's joke at the beginning of this chapter.)

Make Them Feel Welcome

Nothing makes someone confident about his new purchase more than a company that makes him feel like he just bought from friends. Making customers feel **welcome** could be as simple as thanking them publicly online for becoming a customer or complimenting them through Twitter for their good taste. It could also be emailing them the following week to ask how they enjoyed their purchase or following up to ask if they need anything else.

🔍 *Note*

A note about automated surveys: Nothing drives me crazier than an auto-mated email asking for my feedback. While it might be helpful for the com-pany to get info on the purchase, I know the people I interacted with during my purchase will rarely, if ever, see my notes. I'd rather get an email from John, from whom I bought my new sweater, asking me if I like it as much a week later as I did when I bought it. Want to make sure the feed-back goes up the chain? Simply have John cc the boss on the note he sends to me.

So, your goal is to welcome the customer. You're accomplishing some of this while you get his first bit of info, as I mentioned before (asking him about his phone, get-ting his Twitter handle, and so on). Welcoming the customer to your corporate family is one of the easiest ways to grow brand loyalty. Other things I've had clients do or seen other companies do (that work) include

- Offering customers free Internet access for their personal devices while they're on property. To get the access, they first see the company's blog, website, or Facebook page and are invited to join.

- Offering 10% off the purchase immediately if the customer joins the Facebook fan page or follows on Twitter at the time of purchase through his personal device.

- Offering first-time check-in status on FourSquare to anyone who shows that it's his first check-in at that store/location. This usually takes the form of a discount or the like.

Do understand the difference, however, between welcoming and stalking. Customers want to feel welcomed the first time they shop. They don't, however, want to feel stalked. This means don't start emailing them daily or @ replying them on Twitter asking when they're coming back. There's a very fine line between being welcoming and being annoying. The quickest way to lose a new customer (and all his friends) is to cross it.

One basic piece of advice that I don't see enough people take is this: Ask yourself, "If I was the customer and was getting contacted by the company, would the way they're contacting me be okay? Would I mind? Feel bothered? Or would it be just right and encourage me to shop there again?"

Pay attention the next time you feel stalked by a company. See how you feel. How can you improve on that?

When I took out my last car lease, I was asked for my email. I gave it without hesitation, and a few days after I took possession of the car, I got a note thanking me for my business. I thought that was nice of the dealership.

Unfortunately, a week later, I got another email thanking me again and asking me if I'd share with them at least five of my friends who might be looking for a new car so they could reach out to them.

What's wrong with this? Let me count the ways:

1.   Hell no. I'm never going to share my friends' email addresses, especially with a company trying to sell to them.

2.   **KNOW YOUR AUDIENCE.** I live in New York City. I don't even KNOW five people who own cars, let alone are looking for new ones.

3.   To ask a customer to do your work for you is just wrong. Never ask your customers to work for you. By helping them and making them feel welcome, they'll want to do it. But flat-out asking them to do it is simply tacky. If I'm going to help you, why am I paying you?

The end result? I didn't feel welcome.

But what about a way that *does* make you feel welcome?

When I was traveling to Portland, I'd posted on Twitter that I'd just arrived in the Portland airport. I mentioned I was traveling with two other people with whom I was giving a conference the next day.

Five minutes later, someone tweeted the message shown in Figure 6.2.

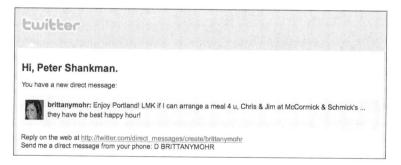

Figure 6.2   *Now this is the way to follow up without making a customer feel stalked or annoyed.*

Okay, seriously. How nice was that? Now granted, I followed her, so she sent me a direct message. But the gist of it is the same.

What if you worked in Portland and created a Tweetdeck column titled "PDX," "Portland Airport," or "landed + Portland" and every time you got a hit, you sent an @reply message to that person saying:

> "Hey (twitter name) – Welcome to Portland! If you'd like to dine with us tonight, we'll give you 10% off your meal! Just show your server this tweet on your phone!"

Not only would you get tons of people willing to take you up on that, but I'd be willing to bet that after a while, you'd get a little bit of publicity out of that, too! And how cool is that?

Make Them Feel Appreciated

Without customers, you wouldn't be here. You wouldn't be reading this book. You wouldn't be doing much of anything. Customers pay the bills. Without them, you're history. Or to quote *Mad Men*, "They can shut off our lights."

Of course, it helps if you imagine me saying that in a gorgeous suit, while smoking a Lucky Strike and sipping a scotch. But anyway, the customers have the power to turn off your lights or to buy you a new bulb. Knowing that, doesn't it make sense to want them to know they're appreciated? Social media makes it easier than it has ever been.

The flip side? You do have to work at it a bit, though.

You constantly need to be thinking of new ways to appreciate your audience. You want to be able to make each and every customer feel appreciated, but you don't want to be automated.

Consider this quick story: A friend of mine used to send personalized emails to all of his friends at least once every few months, in which he'd talk about what he was doing as well as ask about specific details in our lives. We were thrilled to receive them because he took the time to ask specific questions about us personally. It was obviously not a form letter, and we were excited to reply, even if he occasionally asked us for a favor. It was personal, so we were happy to help.

Until one specific email from him landed in our inboxes. He'd accidentally missed a "]" parameter when sending us those "personal" emails. Instead, what we got was this:

> USER24
>
> Hey, USER24 – Doing my usual reach-out. Hope you're doing well! How's that USER24SUBSET1 thing working out for you? What's going on with USER24MATE1? Is USER24MATEGENDER still doing well? Etc... Etc...

And all 200 of his other friends got the same email, as well. Oops. Talk about losing credibility (and friends) really fast.

So, what did we learn from that debacle? Appreciation only counts when it's real. Automated appreciation or a "Thank you SHANKMAN, PETER for your ORDER on DATE" doesn't fly.

Knowing that, I teach clients a few simple rules about appreciation in the social media world.

People Aren't Numbers

Order #2719 doesn't tweet, and delivery 142A doesn't Facebook. But, Joseph Swanson tweets, and Sandy Skinner Facebooks. Customers need to be treated like people, not like numbers.

Automated Outreach Doesn't Cut It

Customers are more than five times as likely to post something online when they feel like they've been taken advantage of, made to play the fool, or treated unfairly than they are if they've been treated well. So right away, the odds are stacked against you. But treating them well (again, like you'd like to be treated) is all you need to start changing those odds.

I work with a big manufacturing company that has multiple sales and distribution hubs around the country. Prior to putting together one major social media plan that all the geographical divisions could share, each division was on its own as to how it wanted to handle its customers after a sale. A few branches went totally automated, meaning they set up a system to automatically email (or worse, call) their customers a week to the second after their purchases, asking them how they liked their product and asking them to fill out a 20-question form (20!) rating the product and the experience on a scale from 1 to 10. They didn't bother tracking on social media or doing anything else. Not surprisingly, their return ratio on the form was an abysmal 5%, and also not surprisingly, the marks from those who *did* fill out the form weren't that high.

Another branch, however, allowed each employee one hour per day where she didn't have to sell. That one hour a day was off the clock and didn't count toward her quota. Rather, that hour was to be used by each employee to reach out to her customers from last week's sales and follow up, personally, in the best way she chose. Some chose email, some chose phone calls, and one older gentleman would actually use the hour to hand-write letters! (For my younger readers, we used to write these things called "letters" on "paper" with a "pen." Then we'd take them to the post office and mail them. It was kinda cool.)

That branch? It had an 80% response rate on follow-up and—more importantly—a 75% referral rate! How's that for pretty cool?

See the difference? It's all about making the customer feel appreciated. Talking to her, asking her questions, and taking an interest is all an act of appreciation. And it's all mandatory if you want to win the game.

I think the key lesson with this client is one specific point: the company lets the employees reach out *any way they want*. For some, that's email. For others, that's Facebook. For others still, that's asking the client if she's on Twitter and, if she is, asking for permission to follow her. Some even use phone calls or hand-written notes. But what it's not, in any capacity, is forced. It's not forced, it's not a requirement that the employees wind up hating, and it is seen through immediately. It's something the employees want to do. For the employees, they love the fact that they get to do this. They love the referral and return rates. And they love making those connections.

I taught the employees in that specific branch how to create Google alerts on their names, so they could track when their customers were talking. They were amazed to find out that they were being complimented online! One employee even called me from home one night so I could explain to his daughter where she could find the alert on his name. (It was adorable.)

Not only were the customers made to feel completely appreciated, but in a roundabout kind of way, so were the employees—*by the customers*! Think about it. Customers appreciating employees for appreciating customers! It's like creating perpetual motion!

As the light bulb went off in this one branch, you know that it spread, and that branch was responsible for some of the key social media guidelines for the company as a whole.

End result? Customer satisfaction is way up. Morale is way up. *Sales* are way up! And the client is thrilled.

Appreciation. It's the new black.

Make Them Want to Return

We've talked about welcoming and appreciation, which are two keys. But without getting them to return (i.e., *loyalty*), you haven't earned anything out of welcoming and appreciation. Loyalty turns one-time customers into customers for life, and it turns customers for life into fans who will shout your brilliance from the rooftops.

Let's look at SeamlessWeb.com.

SeamlessWeb.com is a food-delivery service website. Living in New York City, you have to know three things about food. You have to know how to cook to impress, you have to know how to get the best reservations, and—possibly most importantly—you have to know where to order any type of food at any time of the day.

Here's the thing about ordering food in the city, though: You have 50 billion choices at any given moment. Thai food at 2 a.m.? Done. Pizza for breakfast? Easy. So if you're a restaurant, how do you compete?

SeamlessWeb.com makes it easy. You order food through them. They list all the menus on their site, and they take a cut of the price of the order. Smart service.

But this is NYC. When we come home to our apartments, sometimes we can't even open the doors due to the number of restaurant menus shoved under them.

So how does SeamlessWeb compete with the countless menus delivered daily, to make sure that when I need a pizza from Ray's, I don't reach for my phone, but I reach for a web browser?

All I had to do was try them once. Then they had my email, and they had my address. They could be very annoying, emailing me daily to tell me to order from them, order from them, order from them.

Or, they could use my information sparingly, *when it suits me.* They could market to me *when I wanted to be marketed to.*

When it's pouring out (like, cats and dogs pouring—real rain), I get an email from SeamlessWeb, around 11 a.m., right when I might be starting to feel the initial pangs of hunger. What does the email say to me? Usually something very, very smart:

> "You don't really want to go out in this weather, do you? Order online today only, and we'll take 10 percent off your meal!"

Let's analyze this:

1. It's pouring.

2. I don't want to go outside, and they know this.

3. They're offering me a discount *not* to go outside!

Why would I *not* do this?

By simply putting a little bit of effort into their marketing, SeamlessWeb is taking all the guesswork out of their online marketing efforts. They're making it incredibly simple to stay relevant to me and get me to return by using one of the oldest tricks in the online book—email marketing. And it works.

So, try it. Build an opt-in email list. Use aweber (http://www.aweber.com) or Constant Contact (http://www.constantcontact.com) to start your mailing list.

Make sure it's a mailing list made up of addresses from people who actively gave you permission to market to them.

Then come up with a reason to hit them. And make that reason something other than "Because I want to sell something." Customers who give you permission to market to them are assuming that you're smart enough to give them a reason to read your emails.

You know why the HARO emails we send out every day had such a ridiculously high open rate? Because we send valuable information that the readers *need*. They want the queries in the HARO because it has a higher value to them than the value of not opening the email.

There's your math equation: Is what you're offering worth more to them open than hitting the delete key? Your job is to make sure it is. That's how you get customers to return.

Make Them Want to Share

Mom was right. Sharing *is* caring.

I know this continues to be a theme in this book, but here it is: your job is to get your customers wowed by such stellar customer service that they want to do your PR for you and want to create the PR buzz around your company for you.

They will want to do this for several reasons:

1. The thrill of discovery. We all love to be the cool kid finding something.

2. They want to impress their friends.

3. They want to offer their friends a discount, a deal, or a great service they otherwise wouldn't find on their own.

4. They want to be "that guy" (or girl).

Here are some brief examples of sharing from the Twitter world:

- RT Mashable: "Top Five Ways to get your iPad first."

- Breaking: Lincoln Tunnel Closed to Traffic - Use Holland or Move out of Jersey

- Just walked past Yogurt shop on 58th and 7th - Giving it all away because of Freezer Malfunction!

Each one of those tweets is real. They were all retweeted countless times, and they made the retweeter seem brilliant. He knew something, had valuable information, shared it, and helped people.

Sharing *is* caring.

How can you help your audience share what you're doing for them? Let's focus first on the personal ways. We'll get into the technical ways in the next chapter.

Tweet This!

Put a "tweet this!" button (see http://twitter.com for instructions on how to add a button to your site) that lets people tweet what they just bought from you, what service they just received, or what food order they just placed automatically.

SeamlessWeb.com, mentioned previously, does this with great success.. They have a link labeled "I just ordered from Ray's Pizza on Seamlessweb" with a link to your order. It's easy, simple, and as causal as part of the ordering process itself.

Countless places let you automatically tweet what you just did or post it to Facebook. It's easy, it's free, and it should be a no-brainer when it comes to your first technical output for allowing your clients to share.

Like It

Why not let people "like" every single item on your menu or service list? Each one could be easily "liked" on Facebook, or even just on your site alone. It shows that other people have purchased from you. More importantly, if you use Facebook, you can set it up so that people can see what their friends liked as well.

Loyalty Codes

I believe we're moving toward a world of the one network. By that, I mean it won't be about posting a few things here or posting other things there. There'll be one network, and that one network will let you post everything from what you had for dinner, to your newest baby photos. Everyone you meet will be in your network to some degree, and how you interact with them will determine how relevant they are in your life.

Why does this matter? As you continue to work with your customers and we continue to move toward this one network, *sharing* will become one of the—if not *the*—most important tool in your arsenal. Companies who don't offer easy, multiple sharing links on every page of their site will be eliminated from competition.

We're moving toward a network fueled by trust, powered by recommendation. Without either of those things, your company doesn't stand a chance. Your goal is to grow your company organically by giving satisfied customers the chance to share what you did for them and why they like you. Without those recommendations, you'll be like the company without a website or, back up 50 years, the company without an ad in the phone book.

You don't want to be that company.

So, give your customers something to look for. Something that they can't get anywhere else.

Loyalty codes are spectacular for this. Customers love sharing loyalty codes that not only make them look great by giving their friends discounts, but also reward them with discounts.

Talk to any good web designer, and he can help you create one. It's simply a question of giving the customer his own specific code that his friends can use when they purchase something on his recommendation.

If you're not that technically proficient or don't have a web designer, let customers know they can simply tell you who recommended them. Can you get that person's email, or even a person's name if you're a walk-in store? Any kind of contact info will help. Where did he hear about the code? His friend Mark posted it on Twitter? Be sure to go online and thank Mark.

The technical aspect to what you can do to give your customers the chance to share is limited only by your imagination and budget. In the end, it's quite easy to do. Facebook and Twitter are the obvious ones, but virtually any shopping cart system lets you enter a code to offer a discount. And remember, as long as the margins continue to work in your favor, you can offer those codes anywhere, to any client, in any capacity. Friends, billboards, or coupons—as high tech as we are, and as good as these high-tech methods in this book are, let's not for a second forget the low-tech tips. Sandwich board signs can work just as effectively. Let's not forget the basics.

Buy This, Right Now

The "right here right now" buy is another option. Twitter is famous for answering the question "what are you doing right now?" Well, they've gotten that way because people like to be in the immediate. They like to live in the moment and answer the instantaneousness of it all. Twitter gives them that.

You know what that reminds me of? The impulse buys people make when they shop. You know, the trashy gossip magazine in the front of the store. The pack of gum. The candy bar. These are all impulse buys.

Try this one on for size on Twitter sometime:

> "For the next hour, 25% off everything in our store – Use the code "service" at checkout – Tell your friends!"

We covet what we know. If you're a makeup store and you have people following you who love makeup, they'll tell their friends. If you add to it the time concept—as in, "For a limited time! Call now!"—they'll tell their friends a lot more quickly.

If you're a drugstore, why not offer a special on suntan lotion the week before Memorial Day? Do it as a public service announcement!

> "Don't forget – Summer's coming up – Wear that SPF to take care of your skin! Show this tweet for 20% off all sunscreens!"

Look at that. Not only are you offering a discount, but you're also a nice company who cares! A double win! Go, you!

Try and play with timing, either on Twitter (for immediacy) or Facebook (for longevity, use "20% off now until Friday") or via email (for timed events, use "From May 1 to May 10th – 20% off!").

Either way, you have the ability to reach a much bigger audience when you offer a timed event.

There's an employee I know at a department store who, upon making a sale, doesn't give out his normal store-provided business card anymore. He gives out one that says nothing more than this:

> "You've just been served by @(his username). If I helped, tweet about it! If I didn't, let me fix it before you leave."

I've seen his name mentioned multiple times on Twitter—not only for the "how cool is this" value aspect of it, but also for the "Wow – He was so nice and did such a nice job! You should totally ask for him the next time you go to this department store!"

I also know someone who, instead of including a title and resume on his LinkedIn page, uses this line: "Whatever you need me to be." It's a bit trite, sure, but people remember it.

The goal of sharing is to get people talking. Any way you choose to do that is good. But, obviously, you want them to share because they feel like it's worth it to them, as well as to those with whom they're sharing.

Meet Jason Sadler (see Figure 6.3).

Jason runs a very simple company. It's called "I Wear Your Shirt." His website is at http://iwearyourshirt.com.

This isn't rocket science. Each day, he wears a shirt from a company. He charges based on the day—earlier in the year is cheaper than later in the year. He does this every single day, as he's living his life.

He has an audience of about 25,000 people or so who tune in to his live videos every day to see what he's talking about and whose shirt he happens to be wearing that day. When you stop and think about it, Jason Sadler has taken a simple concept and turned it into a business.

Figure 6.3 *Jason Sadler will wear your company's shirt, for a fee.*

However, Jason soon had a problem. For the first few weeks of this, people tuned in for the novelty concept of it. "Oh, a guy wearing a new shirt. This is funny! Ha," they'd say. But over time, this got to be too old. Why tune in to see some guy in a shirt? Why take time out of my busy day to watch Jason in yet another company's shirt?

What's in it for me?

So Jason got smart. He decided that the audience was right. (The audience usually is.) His job isn't to just wear a shirt. His job is to engage his audience.

Jason's job quickly became to give the customer (in this case, his audience, not the companies paying him to wear their shirts) a reason to come back.

Without Jason's audience, Jason doesn't have a business. Without his audience, why would his customers (this time, the companies paying Jason to wear the shirts) pay Jason to wear their shirts if no one is going to see him? What's the point?

Jason realized this and realized he had to give his audience a reason to come back each day and see his shirts. So he did.

Each client who employs Jason to wear its shirt gives Jason some kind of discount. Be it a monetary one, perhaps a free service, or anything—but something—that he can pass along to his audience.

Sometimes it's a discount; sometimes it's a freebie that they couldn't get anywhere else. Sometimes it's something totally random, specifically made up for the event (for instance, I watched Jason and I got *X*).

But it's always something.

It gives the customers a reason to come back each day and see what shirt this random guy happens to be wearing. And it's working. He has sold out for the past two years.

What can you give your audience? What can't they get anywhere else? What can you offer that will entice them to come back?

Therein lies the value of Sharing.

Recap

Hopefully, this chapter gave you some ideas about the difference between advertising and PR and, more specifically, why both are important and how to implement them.

There's a reason @continental has a loyal following online, and it's not just frequent travelers. They offer incentives to follow them on Facebook and Twitter, as well as on continental.com. They want people to become immersed in Continental. Whether it's giving away free tickets to the U.S. Open or inviting people to guess how much their new 787 Dreamliner weighs, they're asking for involvement.

How will you ask your audience for involvement?

Remember, it's not about automation, nor is it about asking people to do things for you. It's about personalization, customization, and making sure that your customers turn into your audience. They come back time and time again because you're giving them good, solid reasons to do so.

Much like Seamlessweb, or Jason Sadler, or even Kum & Go, you're providing something extra—offering a reason why we should take a few seconds out of our day and pay attention to you. More importantly, you're helping your customers know why they should remember you when they need to make a new purchase and tell their friends about the purchases they just made.

You're using social media as a platform to give your customers something extra, to be different from the norm, to give them something they can't get anywhere else. Something special. Something about which they want to tell their friends.

You're making your customers into addicts. And those are the best kinds of customers to have.

7

Keeping the Addiction Going

Whether you've ever noticed it or not, human beings have patterns. Yes, even you. Chances are, when you wake up in the morning, you have set patterns that you adhere to almost subconsciously, without even being truly aware that you're engaging in them, every single day. For some, it's wake up, coffee, shower, face world. For others, there's a workout involved. For some, like me, feeding two very loud cats enters the picture.

But for the overwhelming majority of us in this country, as well as most other industrialized countries, the first morning patterns include logging on, tuning in, and tuning our minds to "RECEIVE." For more and more of us each day, the morning starts with the intake of information, to make up for the lack of it while we were asleep and lost in dreamland.

Let's look at some other patterns. Back in the '50s, night would come and signal the start of a pattern that involved turning on the TV to watch the evening news, getting into our pajamas, brushing our teeth, and eventually fading off to sleep.

That has changed in the new world. Chances are, your pattern includes plugging in multiple devices so they'll be fully charged the next morning and firing up your laptop or iPad to get your daily dose of news. Instead of being a source for news, the TV is now purely a source of entertainment, thanks to TiVo and other DVRs. But again, until we fall asleep, our receptors are set on "RECEIVE" and our neurons stay in a state of constant hunger, ready to grab whatever new information is coming down the electronic data stream.

One of the most interesting changes in the past 50 years, however, is the level of personalization to which our senses have tuned. Whereas we used to get the same information as everyone else at the same time, the Internet (and social media) has allowed us to personalize what we want to receive, right down to the smallest detail.

Live in NYC but only want the weather for Barcelona? Not a problem. While the nightly news might give you the local weather, weather.com will give you whatever city you want, whenever you want it.

Live in Boston but want to see flight prices between London and Madrid? Piece of cake—just log on.

Personalization has become the keynote behind how we digest our information. Much like Burger King's "Have it Your Way" campaign of the '80s, we can truly have our information personalized to us any way we want it, any time we want it.

The key for us, though—as marketers and businesses competing in this social media world—is to remember that it's not just about giving information. It's about making sure the right information reaches those who want— nay, need—it when they need it. Not a second before, and not a second after.

To paraphrase from the movie Point Break, *"You know how we do it, Utah? By crunching data."*

Your job is to crunch data, find out what your customers want, and give it to them when they want it. Your job is also to use technology to continue to feed their addictions. Let's look at some ways that all different types of businesses do just that.

Ten Rules to Live By

The ten rules of technical social media engagement aren't much different from those of someone dealing drugs—except that social media is legal.

It's time to think like a drug dealer:

1. Anything you put out there has to be something people will try once and want again and again because they believe it benefits them.

2. If the quality isn't good, they won't come back.

3. Yours has to be better and more compelling than anyone else's.

4. You have to develop a "special relationship" with your customers, ensuring that even though they have other options, they always come back to you.

5. You need to offer new value all the time by making it not entirely about the product, but also about new and interesting information customers wouldn't have found otherwise.

6. You must constantly strive to make it an easy experience for the customer. You want a seamless relationship of which the customer feels he needs to be a part.

7. You have to constantly be refining your product to create a better one.

8. When you send your emails, confirm that people want to receive them that way. Text only? Make sure you have a backup version that only sends text, and make sure you offer people the option to receive it that way.

9. You need to be up on what other businesses are doing and have people (or yourself) willing to try competitive products and report back to you.

10. Occasionally, you should offer your customers free product, even though it might cost you a few cents in profit. You're reestablishing their loyalty to you by showing that you're thankful that they're your customers.

And bonus rule, number 11:

11. Never forget that you can have as much product and deliverability as possible, but without the customers, you're dead in the water and another dealer will swoop right in to take your place.

We'll look at each of these rules more closely in the coming sections.

You Want to Hook Your Customers

Rule #1: Anything you put out there has to be something people will try once and want again and again.

When I launched HARO, I thought I could help journalists and sources connect in a better, easier way. What wound up happening is that I offered a service that people found they couldn't live without.

HARO is a simple newsletter, but it's filled with information that helps people improve their businesses. When you answer a HARO query from a journalist, and that journalist interviews you or quotes you, your business gets exposure, which almost always translates into increased visibility and higher sales.

Ever had an amazing sales quarter and then just decide "oh, well that one sales quarter was awesome. I don't need another one, no worries. I'm happy to go back to my previous sales quarter, which was 35% less."

Of course, you haven't.

After you get that first hit—that first, "Hey! We saw you in the *Times!*" call from a friend—you can't stop. It's impossible. You want more. You become hooked. And when that *Times* hit translates into hundreds of new customers and new sales, forget it. Life as you once knew it is over. You can't turn back. You need more, more, more, and you'll do anything to get it.

Or, to be a little less dramatic, you see the value in the HARO email newsletter and you keep opening it as soon as it arrives in your inbox, three times per day. You've seen what it can do for you. You want more.

What can you do for your customers to make them want what you're offering more and more? What value can you give them, above and beyond what you're selling to them? The promise of new information they can't get anywhere else?

Keep in mind also that in this instance, less is most definitely more. You're offering something of value—and it *has* to be of value, *each time you offer it.* So you can't send out crap. Much like the client of the drug dealer, you've set an expectation that what you're going to send him is going to be well worth it. He can't live without that greatness. One guaranteed way to get your customers to leave you for another dealer is to start peddling subpar stuff, be it drugs or information.

If you've given your clients a level of expectation, and that expectation is greatness, failing them is worse than never having them before. This is because they are not only going to go somewhere else, but are also going to tell their friends that you've jumped the shark and are no longer worthy of their time.

Remember MySpace? When the site finally became nothing more than a cacophony of tricked-out pages customizable to seizure-inducing proportions, people started going away. They left their dealer and found a new one. And who was waiting for them? Facebook, with a better, cleaner, and more worthwhile social media experience. Their current dealer's product went downhill, so they found a better dealer.

And while some might question my comparing social media rules with that of a drug dealer, I don't think anyone, for a second, will argue that Facebook is *not* an addiction. Create a better product and offer it with consistent excellence, and you'll create addicts for your business.

Poor Quality = Fewer Returning Customers

Rule #2: If the quality isn't good, they won't come back.

The beauty of social media lies in how easy it is for anyone to create content. The downfall of social media lies in how easy it is for anyone to create content.

Thanks to companies like Constant Contact and Aweber, anyone can create an email newsletter and blast it out to hundreds of people in about five seconds. And it seems like such a good idea at first!

You agonize over your content and spend weeks figuring out what your first email newsletter is going to be. Everything looks perfect. You're going to nail your audience and keep them coming back! It's awesome. You have your opt-in-only mailing list, and after painstakingly reviewing and reviewing the content, you're ready to send it out. Your life has been on hold for the past week as you've crafted this content. You're beyond psyched, and the first newsletter for your business looks great. It has pictures, a photo...it's gonna rock. You're stoked.

Then you send it out, and it is, in fact, *awesome!* People use the "forward this to a friend" link, sending your newsletter out into the stratosphere! More and more people sign up, and within two days, you have triple the users you had in the beginning! New sales are coming in! How happy are you?

Then, a few days after your massive win, as the afterglow starts to fade, a horrible fear settles over you:

"Oh, crap. I've got to keep this up."

Figure 7.1 shows the content and frequency of an email newsletter at the start versus the content and frequency a few months in, as based on new email newsletters I've received in the past year.

Seeing what's happening there? You spend so much time and energy on the first few newsletters that you can't keep it up while still making sure you have the time to...I don't know, *run your business.*

So, what do you do? How do you keep up the quality? For my clients, it comes down to an age-old rule my mom taught me:

"Speak only when you have something to say."

That means producing compelling content *only* when you have compelling content to produce. Don't try to fill the pipeline when there's nothing interesting to share.

One of the quickest ways to get me to unsubscribe from any email newsletter is to send me one that tells me you have nothing interesting to talk about.

While I appreciate that you're trying to reach out to me as a customer, if I'm spending time to open and read your newsletter, I expect, at the very least, to find information worth my time. A sale, an interesting statistic I can share, anything.

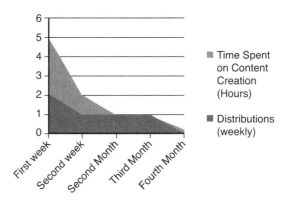

Figure 7.1 *Both time spent on content creation and frequency of new newsletter creation tend to go down over time.*

If you have nothing to say, don't reach out. You want to be known more for compelling content that people anxiously await than for content that is greeted with, "Oh, another crappy newsletter. Delete." Or worse, "Unsubscribe."

Have good content, and send your missives only when you do. This applies to any form of social media, not just email newsletters. Or, as my mom is also known for saying, "Don't speak just to hear your own voice."

Yours Better Be *Better*

Rule #3: Yours has to be better and more compelling than anyone else's.

I have something like 95,000 Twitter followers on @petershankman. But I only follow about 900 people back. It's not because I'm rude, and it's certainly not because I don't care about what they have to say. It's simply a question of time management. If I followed all 95,000 people, I wouldn't be able to keep up with a single one of them. Our brains can only process so much.

Knowing that, your job has to be to offer compelling enough content to ensure that your followers are constantly informed, intrigued, and satiated by the content you produce.

The people I *do* follow, however, have proven themselves time and again to produce compelling content—content that's interesting to me, content I can digest to make my life better, content that offers me solutions to problems I have, or didn't even know I had.

We invite interesting people, companies, and brands into our lives to make our lives more interesting.

I spend the majority of my time on the road. As I'm typing this chapter, I find myself in Barcelona. After mentioning that on Twitter, one of my followers who knows I'm into athletics, posted on my Facebook wall that the European Athletics Championships are currently taking place in Barcelona during the time I'm here (see Figure 7.2).

How awesome is that? Of course, I'm going to attend now. I didn't even know those games were here, especially during the time I'm here! That's spectacular information. It's timely; valuable; and, most importantly, compels me to act.

Figure 7.2   *This bit of information was truly useful and timely. Is the information you send useful and timely?*

Can you find that kind of compelling, timely information for your audience? Well, it's not as hard as you think. You already have an audience who has one major thing in common—they're following your brand. Because it's your brand, you should obviously know what's going on in your industry. People following you are probably also interested in that. Why else would they be following you?

What can you share about your industry, brand, company, or products that is compelling content? Something that makes them act, something that makes them *want to do what you tell them.*

Depending on the type of product or business you're involved with, your content could be compelling in a number of ways. As long as there's something interesting in it, it will keep people interested. Remember: You want them to welcome your content, not roll their eyes and trash it.

Keep in mind also that compelling content doesn't *always* need to link to your company or to a sale. Quite the opposite, actually. The best content tends to keep people interested because it's *not* always about the person or company creating it. It could be a link to an interesting article about your industry or perhaps a funny website that has a connection to what everyone who follows you has in common.

The end result is to create content that people want to see. When you do that, you're feeding the addiction.

Breed Loyal Customers

Rule #4: You have to develop a "special relationship" with your customers, ensuring that even though they have other options, they always come back to you.

Unlike women I've dated in the past, I look at shoes in the following way:

1. They should cover my feet.

2. They shouldn't hurt.

That's about the extent of it.

When it comes to buying a new pair of shoes, though, I have thousands upon thousands of choices. I can buy online at hundreds of stores, or I can walk up the street to the hundreds of stores in Manhattan. I simply don't care enough about my shoes to even give them a second thought. (Dress shoes are a different story, but I digress.)

So, why would someone like me, with that mindset, always go back to Zappos to buy my shoes and never ever go any place else? Zappos has created a special relationship with me and by their actions has turned me into an addict.

Their actions are as follows:

1. They know who I am.

2. They always have what I'm looking for.

3. They provide me with something I can't get anywhere else.

4. They make me feel like I made the right choice immediately after my purchase every time.

When I order from Zappos, I know that I'm going to get upgraded to free overnight shipping each time I buy. I didn't know that the first time. It came as a lovely surprise. Even though I have no guarantees that it's going to keep happening, every time that it does, it's partially expected, yet partially still a surprise to me. And that keeps me coming back.

Zappos constantly surprises me with the little details. They make it so I never have to worry. I know my shoes will be exactly what I ordered, and I know they're going to arrive on time, and the one time they didn't, I got an instant return without so much as a question as to why I was returning them.

They've gone out of their way to differentiate themselves from every other shoe store online or off. And let's face it—for a guy like me, that's impressive. They're just selling shoes, for Pete's sake!

What can you do to make that differential between your company and every other company out there who does similar things?

I call it "Being Burger Guy."

I've worked as an employee at two companies in my life. One was America Online, which was a counterculture blast. I worked there when AOL was just starting out, so it was totally nonconforming and awesome because we made up the rules as we went along.

The second job, the one after AOL, was far from fun. It was corporate culture at its worst. Think Dilbert, without being funny.

Everything at that company (let's call it NOFUNCO) was about protocol and procedure. It felt like people couldn't even go to lunch without having to issue a memo. If you're a fan of Douglas Addams, I was essentially working for the Vogons.

What I learned there, though, was that in a galaxy of bureaucrats, it's easy to be a shining star.

Whenever anyone needed something done at NOFUNCO, they had to send an email requesting the time of another employee. It was miserable. It ensured that no one wanted to meet with anyone else because the meetings were usually just as hellish as the emails requesting them.

So I started doing something differently. I started inviting any employee I needed to meet with out for a burger.

Under the guise of "lunch" (which didn't require a scheduling memo), I'd offer to treat the employee with whom I needed to meet with for a burger. He'd usually jump at the offer of a free meal, and during lunch, I could ask casually ask him for whatever I needed—advice, a sign-off on a project, more hands to help, whatever it was.

About 99% of the time, I got exactly what I wanted. All it cost was the price of a burger. Burger Men are different. They see the world not in meetings and memos, but in fun and in how-can-I-make-your-day-brighter ways.

Zappos does the same thing. I know that when I buy something from them, I'm going to get something extra, whatever it may be. No procedures, no hoops to jump through, just something good that gets me what I need, while giving them what they need (a repeat customer). Everyone wins.

Be different. Be Burger Man.

Offer New Value

Rule #5: You need to offer new value all the time by making it not entirely about the product, but also about new and interesting information customers wouldn't have found otherwise.

Look at the people who share the best content. Those people share with several key values intact:

- It's not always about the product or service they sell.
- They share information that's helpful, not just information to grow sales.
- They share information that other people want to share as well.
- The information they share could be funny, informative, or otherwise, but it's always worth sharing.

Let's check out a company called Blendtec. They make blenders.

Yup. Blenders. That's about it. Exciting, huh? Could you imagine getting an email from them each week? "Hey! We have blenders!" Next week: "Yup. Still have blenders." Following week: "Blenders! They blend things!" Etc. etc. etc. You get the idea.

Yawn to the 10th degree.

Blendtec knew they had a great blender that could blend anything, but again, slicing a cantaloupe into a smoothie can only take you so far. So, they came up with an idea: what if they could blend other things? What if they could blend things tied to current news?

Thus, *Will It Blend?* was born (http://willitblend.com).

It was simple, really. The CEO would take everyday items and see if they'd blend. Blendtec started a YouTube channel, built a website, and pushed out content at least once a week to anyone who wanted to see it.

And in doing so, they created a revolution. Featured on hundreds of news stations and talk shows and on thousands of websites, *Will It Blend?* reached true fame when Blendtec staff stood in line all night to get their hands on one of the first-ever iPhones (see Figure 7.3). And, sure enough, they threw it in the blender—and it blended.

Figure 7.3 *Blendtec's Will It Blend? videos were a stroke of genius.*

Millions of people saw this video and heard about Blendtec. More importantly, Blendtec's sales went through the roof, and people actually *wanted* to see the content Blendtec was producing!

So, what can you do with what you have? How can you build loyal, rabid followers?

One of the keys from the *Will It Blend?* campaign was to keep things *relevant* to the times. When the iPhone came out, they blended it. When Congress passed healthcare reform, not only did they blend it, but they put it on a thumb drive and blended it because the printed version was too big to fit in the blender.

You should be reading the news on a regular basis but also stepping outside your comfort zone: Read different papers, see things from a different perspective, start following blogs you otherwise would have nothing to do with—all to keep up with what's going on and to find new methods to communicate with your audience in an effective, relevant way.

I might not care that Blendtec is blending certain things, but by now, they've hooked me and I don't miss an episode.

And, yes—I went out and bought a Blendtec blender, and yes, it's awesome.

Make It Easy for the Customer

Rule #6: You must constantly strive to make it an easy experience for the customer. You want a seamless relationship of which the customer feels he needs to be a part.

Absolutely nothing drives me crazier (and gets me to unsubscribe to a newsletter or quit a site faster) than not being able to read it because I'm on my BlackBerry or iPad and not in front of a regular computer with a regular email client.

Question: If you have the customer reading your email, tweets, Facebook postings, or blog, why would you go out of your way to annoy her and get her to unsubscribe or turn away?

Yet people do this every day. They use Flash graphics as the first page of their site, so anyone on a device other than the latest laptop can't go past that page. They use tons of high-resolution graphics in an email, not realizing that countless people are reading their emails on BlackBerrys or iPhones in a land of minimal coverage. They make the links hard to find or read and, even worse, make people scroll all the way to the bottom to find them. (Ever have to scroll through 10 pages of text on a BlackBerry? I'd rather chop off my thumbs.)

Why do you go out of your way to cause grief to the very people who pay your bills?

Here are a few key rules:

- You don't control how the customer gets her content. She does.

- Before you do your first reach-out to the customer, know exactly how she likes to receive her information. Just because you have all of her contact info doesn't mean you have the right to use it. (Try to sell me something by calling my mobile, and I'll crush you.)

- Just knowing that your customer likes to receive your content a certain way doesn't cut it. Email? Great. But what type? An email on a desktop is a much different experience from an email on a BlackBerry. There's a reason text-based emails haven't gone away.

- We discussed this before, but it's worth repeating: If your audience isn't where you're trying to reach them, you won't reach them. It sounds simple, but way too many companies have yet to figure this out.

Refine, Refine, Refine

Rule #7: You have to constantly be refining your product to create a better one.

Remember pagers? Once the darling of doctors and the drug dealer set, by the mid-1990s they quickly had become the in-thing to have if you were anyone. With different colors and styles—professional and street, personal and corporate—pagers were where it was at.

When was the last time you saw one?

How about the Newton? Back in 1992, I was the coolest college kid ever with an Apple Newton! So what if it couldn't understand anything I wrote and garbled every message I tried to send with it? It was a Newton! How cool was that?

Or fast forward—a Palm Pilot! I had almost every version available. Then last month, I saw someone using one on an airplane and felt sorry for him.

Technology changes, people. It's a fact of life. Go to YouTube and search for "early cell phone commercials." You'll see what I mean. Search for AT&T's "You Will" campaign from the early 90s. Then laugh. And not just at the fact that Tom Selleck is doing the voice-overs!

So, why is it that so many companies find one thing that works and never bother to refine or change it? "Well, that's the way we've always done it," they say.

A brilliant boss I once had told me this story:

Week 1: Place six baboons in a room. On the ceiling fan, place a banana. Every time a baboon tries to reach for a banana, spray all the baboons with an ice-cold shower. It doesn't matter who reaches for the banana; all baboons get sprayed. After a week of research no baboon in the room will attempt to reach for a banana.

Week 2: Take out one of the baboons and introduce a new one to the room. The first thing that the newcomer will try to attempt is to reach for the banana on the ceiling fan. However, he will deal with encounter force and intimidation from the other baboons because they of course know that his attempt will be followed by the ice-cold shower. After a while, the newcomer will stop attempting to reach for the banana because anytime he does it, he's beaten up by five old-time baboons.

Week 3: Take yet another original baboon out of the pack and introduce a new one. Observe the same scenario. Also, observe the newcomer from Week 2 admonishing the new baboon not to reach for the banana.

Week 4: Same thing. Now you've got three baboons from Week 1 and three new baboons.

Week 5: Same thing.

Week 6: Same thing.

Week 7: This is where it gets interesting. A brand-new baboon is introduced, and none of the original baboons who were in Week 1 remain. However, observe how aggressively the newcomer will be "advised" when he tries to reach for the banana. Notice that none of the baboons currently in the room is aware of the ice-cold shower.

So, why don't they reach for the banana? Because that's the way they've always done it.

Don't be a baboon. Don't be afraid to break the rules and try it a new way! Your customers want you to. They want you to show that you're up with the latest trends and are on the cutting edge.

But they also don't want you to abandon that which works. It's a fine line. Don't cut off text-only emails just because HTML "looks cooler," but don't not offer HTML because you're afraid to move forward from text.

Don't be afraid to cut loose every once in a while, either. Good stories make for great emails. An email doesn't have to always be directly on topic and lead to a sale. But, it does have to be interesting, compelling, and lead people back to you again and again. That's doable.

Facebook is a grand example of this. Every time Facebook changes something, there are riots around the digital world and people threaten to quit, to go somewhere else, to form committees, to kick elected officials out of office, etc.

But do you know what happens? People adapt. Why? Because they don't have a choice. They're on Facebook for life.

 Tip

You're *not* Facebook.

Make sure any changes you implement are accepted by your audience and benefit them, not just you.

Know How Customers Want to Receive Information

Rule #8: When you send your emails, confirm that people want to receive them that way. Text only? Make sure you have a backup version that only sends text, and make sure you offer people the option to receive it that way.

One client I had said, "But everyone will have full HTML email on all devices in the next year." Maybe that's true, but that doesn't mean it will look good, nor does having it equate to ease of use!

I test probably close to 30 phones a year, and on each one, I make sure to read a full-HTML email with photos. I've yet to find one that looks as great as it does on a laptop or desktop. This doesn't mean they don't look okay, but okay isn't good enough when you're trying to give your audience what they want.

Or, to quote Lou Lamoriello, CEO, President, and General Manager of the New Jersey Devils, "Good isn't good enough when better is expected."

Go find a BlackBerry somewhere, and check out an HTML email on it. That's all the proof you'll need.

If you're trying to influence purchasers, your entire operation, from outreach to close, needs to be seamless, easy, and flawless. Do you think I'm going to click "buy" again if the first time I did it, I couldn't tell whether it went through? Never.

Before you send that email or tweet, before you post that blog post or Facebook link, before you open up your new content to the world, you have to check that you've done the simplest thing in the world. Have you tried the link/line/email/purchase yourself?

It sounds simple, but do you have any idea how many companies *don't* do this?

Recently, a friend of mine was launching a new conference. She'd set everything up, broken through for the major launch, gotten the media to cover it, gotten advertising lined up, and launched it.

However, she never bothered to try a test transaction with her own credit card to see if people could register. This would have taken about 10 seconds. It would have been easy to refund her credit card, and she would have been able to fix any problems that came up.

She would have found out that the bank hadn't authorized her credit card processor yet. Instead, though, hundreds of people tried to sign up for the conference the second it was announced, and none got through.

Ouch.

It doesn't take long to do. In the rush to get your content out there, you might forget to do it, and that will cost you every single time. Take 5 minutes; breathe; check all the links, photos, and (most importantly) purchase links; and then take a deep breath again.

Then walk away before hitting Send, or Publish, or Tweet.

I never post anything that could increase or decrease the credibility of my personal or professional brand without taking a deep breath, walking away, doing something else for a few minutes, and then coming back and looking at it again.

Start doing this. You'll find more errors and catch last-minute mistakes this way.

A client was once sending a mass-blast email to all 165,000 of the people on his mailing list. The link drove traffic back to his website for a discount for a new thingamabob. (You'll see why I'm not mentioning who it was in a second.)

He went through the entire email, checked most everything, and hit Send. It took less than 3 minutes for the first complaint to come into his company. How dare they? They'd lost a customer, and if they were lucky, that's all they would lose. That person was thinking of suing.

The calls kept coming, and coming and coming. My client had hit Send, and went out for lunch. By the time he came back, 30 minutes later, he was out of a job.

The problem? The one link to the purchase site peppered throughout the email was off by one character. That one character difference took all the 165,000 members who clicked on it to a hardcore pornography website.

Oops.

Cut and paste, while designed to make your life easier, amplifies your mistakes with each Control+V you press.

Be careful.

Keep an Eye on the Competition

Rule #9: You need to be up on what other businesses are doing and have people (or yourself) willing to try their products and report back.

You know what emails I read religiously almost every single day, as soon as they come out? Before the *New York Times* emails, before even my "Notes from the Universe" emails (http://www.tut.com/theclub/)?

I read emails from my competitors' mailing lists. I check to see what they're doing and how they're doing it. I sometimes even order products from them to test them. If the product sucks, I know I'm doing ok*ay*. If it's awesome, I know it's time to up my game.

It's incredibly simple to do, really.

Go to Gmail and create an email address that has nothing to do with you whatsoever. Sign up. It's that simple.

I know some businesses *that* won't do this. They don't want to know what their competition is doing. They say, "All that time I could be focusing on making my business better." To this, I reply that no matter how good your business is, if you're not monitoring your competition, you're losing to them.

Social media makes keeping an eye on the competition so simple that if you're not monitoring your competition in some capacity, you might want to quit the sport.

Those who don't learn from their competitors are doomed to be eaten by them.

Here's how you can keep up with the competition:

- **Twitter**—Have an alternative account, not related to you. Follow all your competitors and interact with them. Ask questions like any other customer of theirs would. See how (if) they respond. How long did it take? Did the answer satisfy you?

- **Twitter searches**—Every competitor's name should be in a search column of its own. Try Tweetdeck for this (see Figure 7.4). I searched on "sneakers," and got at least three companies with sales in the first line. What else can you do with that?

Figure 7.4   *Use Tweetdeck to follow your competitors.*

- **Facebook**—Create an alternative account, and "like" your competitors. What are they doing that you can do better? Are they posting or actually interacting with their fans? Are they giving things away? Are they inviting criticism and constructive comments, or restricting what people can say? Try interacting with the page and see if the company responds. Keep in mind, this is technically against Facebook's Terms of Service. So if you're afraid of that, perhaps you could have a non-related-by-the-same-name family member do it, and login as them?

- **Blogs**—Have your competitors' blog posts delivered to your email. Use Feedburner (http://feedburner.com) or Google Reader (http://google.

com/reader) to see what they're posting about. You might get some tips on industry trends on which you can expand better than they have, or you might be able to use their ideas to spark ones of your own.

- **Plancast (http://plancast.com)**—Are your competitors posting gatherings? Tweet-ups? Follow their schedule on Plancast, and go to the events if you can. Or if you're well-known, send someone else to go. But get there and see what they're doing.

- **Email newsletters**—Use the nondescript Gmail account you created to follow what the competition is doing. Click through to their links, and see what kind of information they're offering.

- **Search Engine Optimization**—How are you ranking? How are your competitors ranking? SEO is an ongoing process, and while it's not always cheap, it's worth it. That said, there are several tricks and tips you can implement to rank higher on Google. The first and easiest? Post good content to your site often. Google hates a stale website.

- **Google Trends**—If your competition is big enough, see if they're trending on Google and see why by going to http://google.com/trends. Google Trends is probably one of the most underrated tools for social media customer service. Use it. Check out some of the recent trends in Figures 7.5 and 7.6): How can you tie your company into them?

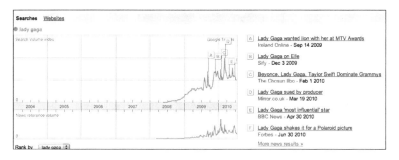

Figure 7.5 *Trend Search for Lady Gaga.*

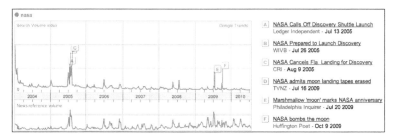

Figure 7.6 *Trend search for NASA.*

Notice how "NASA Bombs the Moon" gets a tremendous amount of play? What do you make that you could tie into that? "20% off sale this weekend, before Doomsday!" Why not? Tongue-and-cheek doesn't hurt now and then!

Keep your eyes open. Opportunity lies all around—especially when it comes to being better than your competitors.

Freebies = Loyalty

Rule #10: Occasionally, offer your customers free product, even though it might cost you a few cents in profit. You're reestablishing their loyalty to you by showing that you're thankful that they're your customers

Drug dealers know this one really well. Rewarding your customers is key to engagement and return. Again, social media makes it easy.

Hardee's Restaurants knows this one really well, too. They constantly monitor social media and respond with free coupons (see figure 7.7) whenever someone says something nice about their brand. In fact, they've even made up specific coupons to give to their admirers—and their detractors. When someone badmouths Hardee's online, their social media group reaches out to him and tries to turn him around. Those coupons are usually a good start, and more often than not, they turn the detractor into a fan.

Figure 7.7 *Hardees rewards customers—particularly those who say nice things about them—with coupons like these.*

Once Hardee's has them, though, they don't stop. They continue to monitor and follow up, and those cute little burger coupons usually go out a few more times. It's easy, it costs very little, and it makes a customer a fanatic.

We're such an email-centric society that the post office can be your friend and really help you to stand out.

When Hardee's sends actual, physical, paper coupons in the shape of a burger, it gets people excited. They want to go and use them. And if they get a free burger, they're going to pay for the fries and drink. And probably bring their family or friends. And probably tell people.

And you thought "come on, first one's free" was just a cool marketing slogan. Well, it is. And it can have seriously good repercussions on your bottom line!

The "first one's free" mentality has been around for years, but adding social media into the mix can boost its benefits to massive proportions. Everyone loves to get something for free.

But as always, there's a kicker: You need to give people something of value *to them*. Reaching out to a vegetarian and offering a half-pound Black Angus burger probably wouldn't do much for Hardee's, huh?

Yet again, it comes down to personalization. This holds true in any industry, whether it be drugs, burgers, or cars. You simply must personalize your reach-outs. First-one's-free doesn't work if it's not personalized. Yes, this means a bit more work for you, but the rewards are there and they're documented. So reach out, by all means—but do it with a point.

Keep an eye out for tweets, posts, or blogs that mention the word b*roken* in combination with a specific product you sell. Is it worth it for you to reach out and offer one of yours as a replacement?

Not only do you get to introduce your brand to a connected consumer who might have never heard of it before, but you also get the possibility that he'll be so thrilled, he'll talk about it—and we all know where that leads.

Reaching out with a point. Try it.

Supply and Demand, Baby...

Rule #11: Never forget that you can have as much product and deliverability as possible, but without the customers, you're dead in the water and another dealer will swoop right in to take your place.

I once bought a new bed from a company that prided themselves on deliverability. They invested heavily in infrastructure, trucks, GPS, route maps, logistics systems, you name it. On paper, there was no one who could beat them for deliverability.

Sadly, they didn't invest as much in their people.

Their delivery people were downright mean. They were rude. They never listened. They never worked with you. They never went out of their way to help you. Quite the opposite, they dropped off their product and were out the door. Need it at a different time? Doesn't matter, call the office. The wrong item? Not our problem, call the office. A rip in the fabric? Nothing we can do, we've got to stick to our schedule.

Needless to say, they didn't last long.

You need to find the balance. Yes, we want the trains to run on time. But if we have to kill people to get there, it's probably not worth it.

Why do people shop from Amazon for the same item they could get at the department store down the street? That's simple: ease of use and trust in the process. We know that if we have a problem, we box it up and ship it back, and they refund our credit card. It's the same product, same price at both Amazon and the department store. But in the end, we want to trust that if we have a problem, it'll be fixed. If the department store has done a better job of proving that to us than Amazon has, we'll use the department store.

Summary

These tools that we're just discovering now have the capability to fundamentally alter not only how we communicate with our customers, but also how we sell.

The biggest problem right now is that too many people see social media as something cool to do and not as a critical component in the sales process.

If the 10 rules in this chapter seem more like sales rules, then *good*! It means you get it. At the end of the day, social media isn't about "cool." It's about selling something. If these tools help you do that, then you're using them wisely. If they don't, then you need to go back, read these rules again, and change your implementation. If each tool you use doesn't have a selling component in it, you're wasting time.

And understand that that doesn't mean all you should do is sell. Quite the opposite—coming on too strong is worse than not coming on at all. Ask anyone who has ever been on a bad first date.

But rather than just selling, each bit of social media outreach in which you participate should have the fundamental message of "yes, we sell things, but we're here to sell to *you*, to make *your* experience perfect, to fix any problems that *you* might have, to listen to *your* compliments or complaints, and to make sure that *you* are 100% satisfied in such a way that you're going to want to tell your friends."

That is the true power of social media. And it's a power just waiting to be harnessed.

Saddle up.

8

Monitoring Your Successes and Failures

The biggest question I get—whether it be from multimillion-dollar clients or a small mom-and-pop store with two employees—is this:

"How do I find the time to do all this 'social media' stuff?"

It's a tough question, with multiple answers. The initial answer I usually give my clients is this: "If you want to find the time, you will."

Seems sort of like a cop-out, huh? It's like saying, "Well, if you want to be a better soccer player, you'll find the time." Or, "If you want to learn Sanskrit, you'll find the time."

Or my personal favorite, "If you want to lose weight, just eat less and exercise more."

Sure. Piece of cake.

If it was really that simple in practice, I'd be an 180-pound Ironman triathlete who spoke six languages and hung out with Renaldo.

Obviously, there's a bit more to it than just "wanting" it. But it's still doable.

You can track social media throughout your day and not have your productivity suffer. You can engage both your fans and detractors in conversation and not lose your ability to do your job, and you can grow your business utilizing social media as a big component and still be able to leave the office at night in time to have a life.

Yes, you, too, can have it all! In just four easy payments of $19.95.... Okay, I'm just kidding about that part.

But seriously, you can. I know, because I've done it. I've taught all my clients to do it. And I'm going to share some of the secrets I've taught them.

But there's one thing to remember—they're not really secrets, per se. They're simply a better way of doing things, using the tools available today. Almost all of them are free, and almost all of them can be tweaked to best serve your interest. The key is just in knowing how.

The tips in this chapter are for everyone. Some might be too basic for you, and some might be too much work. And that's totally fine. We'll start off with the most basic, so if you're ahead of the curve, start reading this chapter about six or so pages in, although, you never know—you might find a tip that works for you. The goal here is to find what works for you. What's right for someone else might not help you at all, and vice versa. It depends on countless factors:

- *What does your company do?*
- *How connected are you, and how often per day?*
- *What do you want to track?*
- *How often do you want to be updated?*
- *How often do you communicate with your audience?*
- *How many sales do you make per day?*
- *How big is your audience?*

And countless other questions. Going through these tips, you'll find the ones that best suit your individual circumstances. And the beauty is that they're fluid. You can change them up whenever the situation calls for it.

Here's one final point: Don't let this stuff scare you. *It is entirely possible for one person to monitor the socialsphere in less than one hour a day for a small-to-medium–sized company. And that hour doesn't have to be all at once. It can be spread out over the entire day, from morning to night. It won't take more than 2–3 minutes at a time to monitor, and a bit more if you're going to respond. But it's not scary, and it is most definitely doable.*

So with that, let's do this thing.

Google Tools

Starting with the granddaddy of them all, we have Google.

What was once a science experiment in a dorm room has turned into the mothership of information. Not a day goes by where Google doesn't affect your life in some way or another. Whether you're getting driving directions, monitoring your brand, or trying to figure out who played the parking attendant in *Beverly Hills Cop 2* (Chris Rock, by the way), Google has fundamentally changed the way we look for, find, and analyze information. And for the majority of what we use it for, it's 100% free.

One other key to keep in mind—Google tends to release their tools as soon as they're "somewhat done." They call them "beta," and it allows them to constantly refine and make them better, while keeping them out there for the public to use. The plus side of this? You get the tools early. There's really no downside, as long as you're okay with knowing that Gmail has been in Beta for five years now. But still, don't let the term "Beta" scare you. It still works.

 Note

> We're just going to look at a few key Google tools in this chapter. However, Google has listed every type of search and utility they have all in one nifty place. Be sure to check in every month or so, as they add more stuff constantly. Start here: http://www.google.com/landing/searchtips/.

Let's start at the easy stuff and work forward from there.

Google News Alerts

Google news alerts (http://www.google.com/alerts) is one of the easiest tracking devices on the planet. It lets you get real-time notifications via any device the second a term you're searching for pops up on the grid.

It's an incredibly easy process: simply enter the terms, enter an email address, and Google does the rest by emailing alerts directly to you whenever someone searches on the terms you specified (see Figure 8.1).

Figure 8.1 *Getting Google alerts is one of the easiest ways to monitor your company, products, or brands.*

Be warned, however: the Googleverse is a big place. Use specific terms to limit your query, or you'll be beyond slammed. In other words, if you build custom swimming pools, I don't recommend you search for "pools." You'll never be able to get into your email.

Use quotes around specific words to limit your search results to relevant information for you. In the example shown in Figure 8.2, I've searched on my name but put it in quotes. Why? Because there are plenty of Shankmans around, and a lot of them are mentioned in articles with someone else named Peter. I don't need to know that Adam Shankman on *Dancing with the Stars* rejected a guy named Peter Vanderfluge. But I do want to know if a story comes out with "Peter Shankman" as that exact phrase.

Figure 8.2   *Be careful setting up the terms for which you want to search.*

This way, I only get searches based on exact terms, not words in different locations in the story.

You can choose what sources you like—Blogs, news, the Web, etc. I recommend choosing All. If you're careful with your specific search terms, you shouldn't get that inundated.

Some people recommend a separate email account where you can get all your Google alerts sent, so you can check it when you want. I *don't* recommend this. Let's face it: how often are you *really* going to check that account? And if you miss a few days or a week, you might come back to something like the example shown in Figure 8.3.

Figure 8.3   *It's easy to get overwhelmed with Google alerts.*

This is bad for multiple reasons, not the least of which is the fact that seeing something this massive would probably cause you to just shut the computer down and run away in fear.

Tomorrow is too late. If you're not monitoring these results in something close to real time, what do you think will happen when you have an angry customer who just wrote a blog post? The best time to staunch the bleeding is as soon as the wound opens. A day later, you've bled out and there are comments all over the blog, not only agreeing with how bad you are, but further calling you out for not responding! That's even worse.

I suggest sending Google news alerts to your regular email. Over time, you'll get really, really good at scanning and acting, or scanning and dismissing, most of the time without even having to click through. Because the email comes with a one-paragraph preview, 80% of the time I can figure out to what the link is related without having to click. This saves me a ton of time.

Additionally, Google has just released "Priority Inbox." With that, you can train Google to know what emails are most important, and it'll throw those to the top of your inbox, no matter when they come in.

In terms of choosing which search terms you want to monitor, obviously your company name is a given. Your company CEO and any other important players in the space should be monitored as well. You'll want to also monitor the name of your company and set up another specific alert for the name of your company plus the word *sucks* or *fail*. I also have one with the initials "WTF." Stands for What the F...," if you didn't already know. Fun dinner time trivia. Make sure you have misspellings of your company name or names of important people in your company if they're easy names to screw up.

News alerts should really be your first line of defense. We'll get into much deeper monitoring, but news alerts are quick, are easy, and do a pretty good job of catching most everything posted in the news, on the Web, and in blogs in close to real time.

Google News (http://news.google.com)

Do a 5-second scan of Google News (http://news.google.com) every morning and, if you have the time, a few times throughout the day. Not only do you get a one-pager glimpse of what's going on in the world, but you also can ideas about social media promotions you can implement that tie in with what's going on in the world. (Remember that a PR or social media stunt for the sake of a stunt is pointless; you want concrete, actionable results, and tying what you're doing into a news hook can give you just that.)

As I write this, I notice through Google News that Snookie from the MTV show *Jersey Shore* was arrested for being drunk in public after she fell off a bicycle she was trying to ride. If I ran a company that had any connection to bike riding, the outdoors, or anything, it'd be very simple to post a "SOS – SAVE OUR SNOOKIE" campaign on our Facebook fan page, where anyone who came in and purchased anything got 10% off, or some similar discount, based on the news of the day.

Thanks to the news, you could technically produce a special a day, if you wanted to. I tell my clients to save them for really fun promotions, things that you can do that won't just generate sales, but perhaps tie in some media promotion for you, as well.

Google Blogsearch

Let's assume you just want to hear from the blogosphere, and not the mainstream media. You can search only blogs through Google Blogsearch (http://blogsearch. google.com), as well.

This is helpful when you want more of the voices of the people, as opposed to what mainstream media is reporting. Granted, there will be overlap, but I recommend checking Blogsearch at least once a day. Additionally, if you've chosen All from your sources in news alerts, you'll get updates from that, as well. Still, Blogsearch comes in handy when you want to find previously published pieces, background on competitors, or other similar information.

Twitter

Let's look at Twitter and utilizing it to monitor the conversation about your company. Do this several times a day, and it shouldn't take more than a minute and a half each time. Your goal here is the quick scan. You want to figure out what, if any, is the current sentiment on your company, your brand, and your competition as a whole. I personally use Tweetdeck to do this, but I'm also a fan of Hootsuite (http://hootsuite.com) as well.

Once you've set up either platform, you can start monitoring mentions of not only your Twitter name, but also of your company, your competitors, and your brand as a whole. Simply set up search columns in whichever program you choose and follow it several times throughout the day.

I'll talk a little more about how I use Twitter while mobile, but don't overlook that you can check your corporate brand at red lights (but don't text while driving!), while waiting in line at the bank, or anytime you have 30 seconds of downtime. I use UberTwitter for that because I have a BlackBerry (http://www.ubertwitter.com). Again, though, use whichever tool works for you. Ubertwitter is a great time-saver!

Twitter has lots of other uses, in addition to 24-hour monitoring of what the world is saying.

I'm a huge fan of sharing photos on Twitter. I encourage brands big and small to do this, as well. If tweeting is sharing what you're doing, sharing photos via Twitter is showing the world what's going on where you are. And that has tremendous value to your audience.

Coach (the expensive handbag company) does an amazing job with this. They send photos via Twitter from all their events (see Figure 8.4). This accomplishes several key objectives. First, people get to see the events instead of just reading about them. Second, Coach customers get that "special" feeling of attention. And lastly, the company shows that they know how to have a good time and show a great image to the world.

GrillGrate is another example. GrillGrate is a small company that showcases its grill accessories in a cool way—with good food! Figure 8.5 shows what I mean.

You don't have to be a huge company with a massive marketing budget to showcase yourself. A BlackBerry or an iPhone along with a Twitter account will do the same thing.

Finally, a note on contests. A client, Haworth, makes office furniture. While you wouldn't think that's the most exciting thing to follow online, you don't know Haworth. Over in Holland, Michigan, they're always willing to try something new and exciting. They recently launched a line of chairs called Very.

Figure 8.4   *Coach makes use of Twitter to help draw people to their events.*

Figure 8.5   *GrillGrate uses good food to showcase its line of grill accessories.*

The contest was simple: Post a "very" cool picture of you and your Very chair (www.haworth.com/verytweet). Haworth then took the best photos and posted them on Twitter (http://twitter.com/haworthinc). Word got out, and people started posting. Following are a few examples of those posts:

- Photo is called "Very Reflective." We just think VACATION. http://plixi. com/p/34244851

- I promise to be a VERY good chair. I promise to be a VERY good chair. http://plixi.com/p/34071130

- A Very special tweet & photo to celebrate a Haworth staffer's wedding this weekend! http://plixi.com/p/32852964

- RT Gensler's James Bond Museum http://bit.ly/bdIfty. So cool - maybe Very contest can help - http://plixi.com/p/32501383

This generated not only additional traffic to both Haworth's Twitter and Facebook pages, but also talk from the local social media press and even a compliment from Haworth's biggest competitor:

Hat tip to @Haworthinc for these "Very" creative promo photos: http://plixi.com/p/ 32501383

Total cost? $0.00. Increase in sales? To be determined, but as of this writing, it's believed so.

It's incredibly easy to put "follow us" buttons on virtually every page of your site. Hey, if they like you, they'll follow you. Why not give them an easy way to do it?

Three additional notes before we move on from Twitter:

- Let's remember that Twitter, in the end, is simply a pipe for distributing information. And like pipes in the past, they occasionally go away and get replaced by other pipes. Use Twitter, but don't put all your eggs in one basket. What happens if Twitter doesn't figure out a way to make money? Unlikely, but not impossible. What happens if something cooler comes along and takes its place? And what if your entire marketing budget is tied up in it? Think it can't happen? America Online. MySpace. Pointcast. The stories go on and on. Be very careful. Embrace the technology, but don't marry it.

- Don't overtweet. Be careful with what you put out there. Post interesting tidbits of information that will excite your audience and leave them wanting more. Post valuable information that your audience will want to share. Remember that the value of Twitter lies in the retweet.

- Finally, and this should go without saying, don't tweet drunk or angry.
  In fact, do what I do. When I know I'm going to an event or a party
  where there might be alcohol involved, I won't tweet at all. I'll bring a
  cell phone, but it's a phone that isn't connected to Facebook or Twitter.
  Trust me on this: Nothing that you *absolutely must tweet right now at 1
  a.m.* is ever as important at 7 a.m. the following day. Please believe me
  when I say that. I speak from prior experience.

Facebook

You know, five years ago, Facebook was thought of as "a place where nerds go for
study buddies." How the times have changed.

I'm not going to bore you with what to do on Facebook, and I'll talk about how I
use it later in this chapter. I will offer you the following rules, though. These rules
tend to work for my clients.

- I've yet to meet anyone who's friends with a company. You don't go to a
  bar and introduce your buddies to your new friend IBM, so why would
  you create a personal Facebook page for your business? You shouldn't,
  and if you do and Facebook catches you, they'll delete it without warning. That's what "Like" pages are for.

- "Like" pages have great tracking tools attached to them—from the initial "this image has XX views," to the weekly status updates you'll get
  from Facebook regarding your fan page. This is *real* statistical data on
  which you can immediately act.

- I work with my clients to get them to understand the differences in
  their week-to-week Facebook "like" numbers and what they mean. In
  the simplest logic, what you're posting obviously relates to the people
  fanning you. It's Marketing 101, but you'd be surprised how many people don't make the connection. Simply keep an eye on your numbers, as
  you go from day to day or week to week. Are you posting something
  that generates a lot of comments or controversy? See if your numbers
  have risen or fallen a week later, and adjust or continue accordingly.

- It's quite simple to put a "Like us on Facebook!" button on your site,
  Facebook gives you tons of pre-made buttons. See the right side of
  www.shankman.com for some idea as to how I do mine.

- Additionally, try to monitor how people get to your corporate page.
  Think of it as random quality assurance testing. Take one or two people
  who have joined your like page in the past week, and shoot them a
  quick thank-you note offering them a code for some type of discount

or freebie, while also asking them how they happened to find your like page. Personalize it—you don't want it to be a form letter—and act on the results. If you're seeing like page growth from in-store promotions or similar, increase those! If more from other places, consider shifting your budget around. Reaching out to your fans via this quality control method is a simple thing and a great way to track where your audience comes from and why they're with you.

- Create a separate account to look at your fan page as just that: a fan. It's easy to look at your page in "master" mode where you see everything. But check it out as a fan, and you'll notice a world of difference. You don't necessarily see all the fan comments, so you just see your comments—the page's comments. How does that look? Too much? Too little? Can you tweak the layout or formation of the page to be more user-friendly? Prettier? Figures 8.6 and 8.7 show two different design examples of Facebook pages: neat and pretty, and tricked out and hot.

✉ *Note*

Whichever design style you choose, know that your goal is *interaction*. You're not just selling; you're interacting with your audience. Make sure you never forget that.

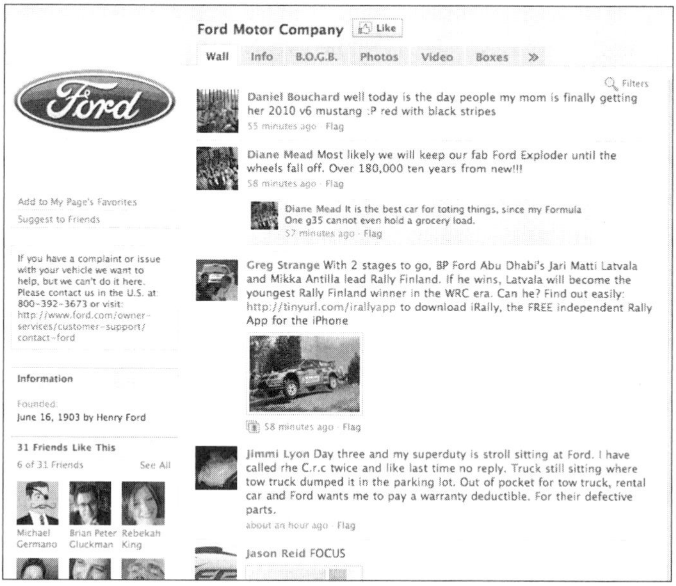

Figure 8.6 *Neat and pretty.*

Figure 8.7 *Tricked out and hot.*

- It's easy to create amazing Facebook pages that pop, no matter what your budget. We work with several companies that have stellar track records for building spectacular pages. Ask around, and ask other brands whose pages you like who designed theirs.

- Don't forget that any photos you post on Twitter, Facebook, or the like can and should transport over to your company blog. Spend 5 minutes a week backing up any media you've posted to Facebook, so in case the worst happens, you'll have backups.

▶ Caution

Remember: Once your content is posted on Facebook, you don't own that copy of it, and you have no claim to it if Facebook suddenly decides to shut down your page or delete your account. Getting in touch with human beings at Facebook is a long and convoluted process. It's worth taking a few minutes to read the Facebook terms of use at http://www.facebook.com/terms.php?ref=pf. You should be aware that Facebook has the option of shutting down your page with absolutely no notice at any time.

- Ask yourself what would happen if you woke up one day and your Facebook fan page was gone. Would you have an alternative way to communicate with your audience? Make sure you get as much information on your followers off of Facebook as you can. Or, at the very least, make sure you're always offering directions on how they can find your blog and contact you in other ways.

- Having multiple channels (Twitter, Facebook, etc.) and having at least one that you own (your blog, your website, an email list, and so on) is a guaranteed way to make sure you can always keep at least a decent portion of your fan base if the worst were to happen and you woke up without one means of communicating. (It's along the same line of why airplanes can fly with half their engines gone.)

Email Marketing

Once the highlight of any social marketer's life, email marketing has taken a backseat to the quick-hit social tools like Facebook and Twitter. A backseat role is a place email marketing doesn't deserve.

It has been said countless times that email is the original and one true killer application. I agree. I built a multimillion-dollar business based on three text-based emails per day. I would even suggest that email, when properly managed, is the #1 tool in your arsenal, above all the other social outreach playthings.

Here are email's pros:

- You have pure, unrestricted access to your audience (which you must use with caution, but you still have it).

- You own the content, and it remains yours (as opposed to what we discussed earlier, where Facebook or Twitter can kill your account with absolutely no prior warning).

- You have control over what you send, when you send it, and how often it's sent.

- Unlike Facebook or any other social site, email is the most unfiltered access to your audience there is, short of a phone call. Everyone has email, and everyone has immediate access to it.

- Email is interruptive. Again, with great power comes great responsibility, but it's real and in your face.

When HARO launched, we needed to look for an email service provider that had several things:

- **Ease of use**—We needed a service to which we could post the content and it would send. We didn't want to worry about coding or HTML.

- **Good relationships with major Internet service providers (ISPs)**— Sending an email to 20,000 people isn't effective if your service provider is thought of as a spammer and only 1,500 of your emails get through.

- **Good customer support**—When we had questions, we needed immediate answers.

- **Good price**—HARO launched on my couch; we didn't have any funding at all.

The initial answer, and one that served us well for our first 18 months of hyper-growth, was aweber (http://www.aweber.com). They have a very simple interface that allows you to be up and running almost immediately, and the ease-of-use worked for us.

Other great options include Mailchimp (www.mailchimp.com) (with a really cute monkey that makes you smile every time you open the site,) and Blue Sky Factory (www.blueskyfactory.com). You'll need to experiment a bit to determine which ones work best for you.

Considering we were sending three emails a day, five days a week, to an ever-growing audience, the price point was right as well: $59 per month, with no extra costs.

One of the keys to a successful email campaign is simply knowing what to send and when to send it. Holding back might be the most underrated tool in the email world.

Email is personal to people, much more so than any other form of social communication. Look at it this way: getting someone's email address from her for marketing purposes is a privilege. Try really hard not to abuse it.

There are only two acceptable ways of securing someone's email address:

1. She physically gives it to you during a sale or transaction. If the sale occurs in person, ask her if it's okay for you to occasionally email her.

2. You receive it during an online transaction. If you receive it online, confirm with checkboxes that it's okay or not okay for you to occasionally email her.

That's it. There are no other ways. Don't buy lists. Don't add people from your address book because you think they'll want to hear about your company.

That's spam. It's illegal. And more importantly, it's tremendously not cool. As soon as you're thought of as a spammer, forget it. You'll spend the rest of your life trying to remove that connotation.

Make sure it's clear for what you're having people sign up. If it's only emails from you, make that clear. If it's from 3rd parties as well, have another checkbox that allows/disallows that. And for the love of all things, do NOT pre-check the boxes. Let your users check them. Pre-checking the boxes to "Yes" guarantees that I won't be signing up for anything you have to offer. It's simply rude.

When you have your list ready, decide how many times you'll send content and stick to it. For my clients, it's when we have enough to say that warrants the interruption. I suggest you do the same.

Only you can tell what type of content to include. Make a call to action mandatory, though. Offer some kind of discount or special in each email, but on the same note, don't make it all sales-y. Make sure you put in some actual content.

Unlike short messages on Twitter or Facebook, people open email expecting to read. Come up with a good story, an idea, something that makes it worth clicking. It could just be nothing more than an interesting quote you heard that resonates with your audience for some reason, but find something. Don't make it just about the sale.

The biggest complaint we got when we would send the HARO had to do with the frequency of the sends. Keep in mind that we were sending media requests that were time-sensitive. We had to send multiple emails per day—an email going out at noon for a 10 a.m. deadline didn't help anyone.

You, on the other hand, don't have those issues. Chances are, you're not sending emails that have to be answered in an hour. So you're able to space your emails in a way that doesn't bother your audience. And trust me, they'll be quite vocal if you bother them. Simply put: they'll unsubscribe.

Your goal should be an even flow of sends, spaced as far apart as possible, without losing your audience's interest.

Another possibility, which we've used with great success, is specific sends on specific days. For example, "10% Off Fridays!" or "Fashion Thursdays!" or something similar. By cultivating an air of anticipation, you get your audience to hunger for the emails. When the HARO is as much as 5 minutes late, the Twitters start: "Where's the HARO?" We've cultivated that air of need within our audience. What can you do to cultivate the same thing?

Southwest Airlines does it very well with their "Ding!" fare sale emails, as does Continental and United. We're trained to know when those emails are going to arrive, and if we want a cheap, quick getaway, we're at the computer when they arrive.

How are you going to create that level of anticipation and want throughout your audience?

An Example of Email Marketing Done Right

Here's how Scott Jordan, founder of the wildly successful SCOTTEVEST line of technologically enabled clothing (http://www.scottevest.com), uses email mixed with social media, online advertising, and a solid commitment to customer service to benefit his sales and increase audience interaction. For him, the key is that the SCOTTEVEST is an additional piece of baggage or a jacket that carries everything, instead of a bag or additional piece of luggage. Full disclosure: I'm a huge fan of the SCOTTEVEST line, so much in fact, that I joined their advisory board several years so.

So... Based on what Scott's brand continues to build:

- SCOTTEVEST leads the audience down a "pain funnel," sympathetically recounting why extra baggage fees are unfair and fanny packs look goofy, and reminding the audience of the frustration they will face the next time they travel (converting the idea of their need into a visceral reaction).

- They speak to audience members specifically when they are in a buying mode, such as through search advertising. This is the nexus of need and desire.

- In advertising, and especially in email marketing, they draw in the audience with the one-two punch of good, curiosity-sparking, crave-worthy content and one-day-only X%-off sales. Whether someone "desires" or "needs" the product, he is able to justify his purchase to himself.

- They maintain contact with previous customers (via email, social media, print catalogs, etc.) to give them compelling reasons to come back. A desire only requires a reminder to become real, whereas a need requires proof and justification. New products and new ways of presenting items (*such as their magazine pocket being spun into an iPad pocket*) all add up to fresh sales. (What can you do to keep up with the times?)

- SCOTTEVEST has the goal of being that little voice in their customers' heads that reminds them of what they want/need. SCOTTEVEST utilizes the technology of retargeting to do this by showing online ads specifically to people who have visited their site. "Whether it's due to a need or a desire," says Jordan, "that little extra push can convert people from interested audience members into actual customers."

Finding the Time to Monitor Social Media

Finally—How do you find the time?

That's my most favorite question of all, as I stated in the beginning of this chapter. Instead of explaining to you how it's possible, I'm going to take you through a day in my life, showing you how I monitor social media in addition to everything else I do for a living.

This might be over-the-top for you, or it might not be enough. It all depends on what works for you, obviously. But the bigger picture that I'm trying to get across here is that it doesn't require full-time dedication to the project—or rather, it doesn't require you to give up the rest of your personal and professional life to monitor your brand, the conversations, and what's going on in general out there.

You can, in fact, do it all. Here's how I start my day:

1. Wake up at 5:00 a.m.

2. Upon waking up, I turn on my BlackBerry (Yes, I turn it off when I sleep. Really, what's pressing at 3:30 a.m. that you can't work on at 5:00 a.m.? And if someone really needs me, he'll have my home number anyway.)

3. While still lying in bed, I hit UberTwitter on my BlackBerry and search both on "@replies" (this is for mentions on my Twitter handle) and as on my company name to analyze anything that has come in or broken over the course of the night while I was sleeping.

4. As UberTwitter is loading, I check my email. Any Google news alerts get checked first, as well as anything urgent from clients overseas.

5. For the next few minutes, I scroll back and forth between UberTwitter and http://news.google.com, looking to see what's going on in the world. Between the two sources, I pretty much have a good handle on what are going to be the hot buzzwords and keywords of the day. This is great if I decide to produce a sale or an event later through social media and tie it into the news of the day.

   So, for the first update of the morning—including social media, news, and pop culture—the total time is between 4 and 6 minutes.

6. Next, I go for a run, hit the gym, or the like. Over the course of the previous evening, iTunes has automatically downloaded several podcasts to my iPod. When I go for my morning run, swim, or bike ride, I catch up on information, which is received the way I prefer to get it. Remember

how I mentioned earlier in the book about making sure your clients get their information they way they want it? Well, never forget that you're a client, too. I know I'd never visit ZDnet, CNET, or the BBC websites during the day—I'm way too busy. But to get all my information while I'm sleeping and then listen to it during the first hour of my day works for me. It's how I like to receive information. There is no schedule anymore. There's only real-time when it suits you. If you don't believe me, ask any sixteen year old the last time they watched anything on TV according to the channel's schedule vs. TiVo.

So, I spend an hour getting sweaty, but also getting a little bit smarter. And that's where it gets beneficial.

By the time I finish my run, I have in my head, from my workout, no less than five interesting stories worth tweeting or posting on Facebook. Some might have to do with my industry, some might be random, and some might just be funny. But regardless, I can then *provide value* to my audience by posting these over the course of the day. They're interesting, they're informative, and they're not overly (if at all) self-promotional.

Total time: one hour (because I'm not a fast runner by any means; your time might be shorter).

Finally, my day starts. My computer has the following running at all times:

- Tweetdeck

- Facebook

- Google Alerts window

- Adium (http://adium.im), which is a full instant message client that houses AIM/Gtalk/Yahoo/MSN/and so on

- Skype

That's my control station. Because I'm a bit of a geek, I actually have it lined up in my office as shown in Figure 8.8.

Obviously, you don't have to to such extremes. But whatever works for you, those are the applications I have up. I keep the volume just above mute so that I can hear specific alert tones I have assigned to specific senders, direct messages, and so on.

Despite my love of my couch and social media monitoring station, I'm usually out of the office more times than I'm in it. So for that, I rely on my BlackBerry and EVO 4G. I carry more than one device because I'm a geek. You don't need to.

Figure 8.8 *My control station.*

On my BlackBerry, I use UberTwitter to monitor information on a regular basis. What I like about UberTwitter is the ease with which I can search for @replies, as well as search terms of my choosing, all while waiting for the light to change or the plane to taxi to the gate.

If you're not using Google Apps for your email hosting, I strongly recommend it. At $50 a year per user, it's well worth it. Tons of times I've needed an address, a person's info, or a particular bit of information from a meeting. With Google Apps, I can simply use the Gmail for BlackBerry (or for Android) tool, and it syncs with my corporate email—no hassle at all. From there, I can use Google's really amazing email search functionality. It has saved my life on more than one occasion when I was down to one bar on my BlackBerry.

Speaking of battery life, you should keep an extra BlackBerry battery shoved in your coat or purse (fully charged, of course). The charger and a small $5 roll-up charger will be the best investments you've ever made. Remember the rule of ABC for mobile electronic devices: **Always Be Charging**.

Another way I use social media on-the-go is to constantly check in on Foursquare wherever I am. This is a great way to really get out there in front of your audience, as it were.

For example, say you're the PR manager of a small business. Create an account on Foursquare, as you, and check in wherever you go during business hours. As more of your customers and fans start to friend you on Foursquare, they'll also notice what you do, and they just might wind up in the same place as you. When they do, it's a great way to meet them in person and make them feel special.

Laugh if you want, but the odds of that happening, although small, are increasing every day. I had a lovely chat with a woman last month who's a huge fan of HARO. Where did this happen? On the M-6 bus, of all places, headed down 7th Avenue. She saw that I had checked in and looked up to find me sitting there, reading my BlackBerry. She came over and said hi, and we talked for 20 minutes in traffic. The next day, she emailed me and asked me for HARO advertising rates. And the day after that, she bought six ads for her company. One quick conversation on a bus turned into a $9,000 advertising buy. Not too bad for a free application that told someone I was on a bus!

Installing the Facebook application for your particular device will prove useful because you're able to download all the status updates of your friends and customers and respond whenever you'd like—on a train, while stuck in the subway, and so on. It doesn't matter if you don't have service because you can simply respond at your leisure, and the system will send as soon as it reacquires a network. This is an excellent way to keep the conversation going when you have 5 minutes of downtime.

Here are a few more tips:

- Carry a camera (and a video camera, if you can) *everywhere*. You never know when you're going to see something amazing that you can post on Facebook, Twitter, your blog, and so on, and that can generate conversation. Most good mobile phones have both built in, and the quality is getting better and better in every generation.

- Example: As I was coming off a plane last week in Peoria, IL, I saw a serviceman returning home from Iraq. I let him go first, and sure enough, his wife was waiting for him with his five year old daughter, outside the gate. I grabbed a photo of the giant hug he gave them both, and uploaded it to Facebook from my Blackberry, with the hashtag "#thankasoldier." That photo received more than 50 comments in five minutes.

- Use services such as 12 Seconds (www.12seconds.tv) to upload quick-burst video to your audience, giving them more interactivity. For longer videos, invest in a good-quality camera. Never underestimate the value of a decent video for sparking conversation. Sites such as Vimeo (http://vimeo.com) and YouTube (http://youtube.com) have shown to be excellent places to start a video collection, and the ability to embed on your own sites or social stations makes the process seamless.

- One of my employees loves updating me with what's going on with the company when he's driving home. But he knows I only like email and don't like to spend lots of time on the phone. He also knows he can't type while he's driving. So he found a solution: He uses one of several different services that allows you to call a phone number, record a message, then say the email address you want to send it to. Next thing I know, I get two minute mp3s in my email, that I can listen to as I'm checking my email. Everyone wins. Check out iTalk, or countless others.

At the end of the day, these are simply suggestions. Some might be way too simple for you; others might be something you didn't think of until you read it here and thought, "Hey, that could work!"

The goal here is what works for you. I know I'm a geek, and I know what works for me. I like to be connected almost all the time. This might not work as well for you. If so, no worries, simply adapt my suggestions to what does work. Use your own. In fact, I want to hear them! Got some good ones that make you more productive? Email me – peter@shankman.com - Let me know.

In the end, it doesn't matter if that's one tweet a week to capture your audience's attention, like a museum in New Hampshire does, or several "Instasales" on all forms of social media each day, like an airline in Europe does. Trying to do what another company does simply because they do it is pointless. Do it because it works for you.

But, if nothing else, do *something*.

9

Putting It All Together: What Did We Learn?

I once had a boss, the general manager of the New Jersey Devils. He had a sign above the Devils' locker room. It said simply, "Good isn't good enough, when better is expected."

That always stuck with me. For whatever reason, in life, we tend to do a lot of work via the creed of "it'll get by." I never truly understood that, even if I've done it, too, from time to time. But no matter what the cause (I'm tired, I got to bed late, I have to leave early, my keyboard is broken, my desk chair hurts, my hairline is receding...), we still seem to do it.

Why?

If you're still reading this, you've obviously wanted to improve. You've obviously decided that "the norm" is for everyone else and you want to be better.

Good.

But here's the problem, as well as I can see it:

I give keynotes to thousand-person conferences on a regular basis. I tell them the so-called "secrets" of social media, customer service, and marketing. These secrets aren't really so secret at all. They're simply what has worked for me, what has worked for the companies I've run, and what has helped those companies generate tremendous revenue and excellent prices when they're sold.

They're not secrets, and while they're not monumentally difficult, they're also not easy. They're fun, but they're a lot of work. They're answering phones when they ring and not letting the calls go to voice mail. They're canceling the occasional weekend plans because work intrudes. They're placating a pissed-off customer after she has screamed at you because you believe she deserves the best.

It's a lot of things that we might not always like.

So I tell these stories, and then I wish everyone good luck and send them out into the world, hoping that perhaps they'll do what I recommended. Or if nothing else, they'll at least try it.

Then life goes on, and the sun continues to rise and set. Mostly, I never hear from anyone in the audience as to whether they implemented anything I advised.

✉ *Note*

If you implement anything I've recommended in this book, please email me (peter@shankman.com) and let me know how it went!

But then, every once in a while, I get an email letting me know that someone tried something and what the results were. And those few-and-far-between moments make it all worth it.

When the convention and visitors bureau in a small state somewhere in the Midwest emails me and says they bought 10 flip-cams to give to frequent visitors and saw their Facebook "likes" go through the roof and, more importantly, tourism measurably increase, I read those emails and jump out of my chair and do a little happy dance.

🔍 *Tip*

Never become so serious or so "professional" that you can't allow yourself to do a happy dance. What is a happy dance? Google "Happy Dance" and "Snoopy."

Why am I doing a happy dance? Not because they took my advice and it proved correct (although that's pretty freaking cool in itself) and not because the advice I gave produced *measureable results that beneficially increased someone's business*, but simply because the majority of people who go to conferences, read business books, or listen to so-called experts never actually implement even 1/100 of the advice given to them.

That's a whole other issue. Why the heck are we going to all of these conferences if we're never going to implement anything we learn at them? Are we really learning anything? If a tree falls in the forest...

Look around the country. There's no doubt that we have a problem with obesity in America, right? Everywhere you look, you see it. And you can't tell me with a straight face that there's a single overweight person out there who *doesn't* know that decreasing the amount of food he eats and increasing the amount of physical activity he gets will help him lose weight. We all know that. Want to lose weight? Diet and exercise.

Except knowing it and implementing it are two completely, totally unconnected things, and as a society, I believe we have a problem interlocking the two. We know we shouldn't have that triple cheeseburger with bacon and mayo for lunch every day because it's not good for us. But it tastes really good, and it tastes better than that healthy salad with cucumbers and balsamic vinegar. So we eat it. And we get fat, even though we know what to eat to prevent us from getting fat.

It's a lot of the same thing with marketing and social media, sadly. We know what we have to do. We can learn what works. We can listen to the so-called experts. We can read the case studies, and we can figure out how to apply those case studies to our companies and brands.

Then why don't we?

I have a theory here. I believe that for the most part, we don't for two reasons.

1. It's hard.

2. It's not the way it has been done before.

It's one thing to convince ourselves to do something hard. It's something else to do something hard that we've never done before and something for which we don't have a guarantee of success.

But that, my friends, is how *change* happens.

Remember my story about the baboons, the ceiling fan, and the bananas (refer to Chapter 8)? Don't fear change.

The World of One Screen

I believe one of the biggest problems facing us right now in the world of social media, customer service, and business as a whole is that we're *not looking far enough ahead into the future.*

Imagine this, if you would.

I was brought in to speak to a big Fortune 100 company the other day. I was asked to speak to them about social media, which is standard practice, right? They wanted me to explain how they could get all their teams working together on the same page and what practices I've used in the past with other companies (and my own) to make the process seamless so all the different departments knew what the others were doing.

I naturally assumed they were talking about, you know, the customer service group interfacing with the marketing team, who would talk to the PR team, and so on. Imagine my shock when I got to the room and was introduced to more than 60 people from four different teams. Can you guess what the teams were?

- The Web Team

- The Mobile Team

- The Desktop Team

- The Online Team

Yup. They actually had four different teams simply devoted to the different ways a person could get online to reach them. They didn't even think, for a second, that social media needed to have customer service, PR, marketing, and so on involved.

As I was sitting there wondering if I had anything in my laptop bag that I could ingest to make me throw up so I didn't have to talk to them, it occurred to me: this was how they saw social media. They looked at the different ways a person could interact with their company—not from the concept of who the customer needed to talk to at that moment, but rather from which device the customer happened to be using at the time.

If I had been a rapper at that moment, I'd have been DJ Shortsighted.

The fact is, we need to stop looking at different screens as the end result. In 24 months, it's not going to matter how we access a company. It's not going to matter whether we call, log on from our mobile device, get online through our desktop, or use a kiosk at the airport.

We're moving very, very quickly to the World of One Screen.

The World of One Screen (WOS) is a magical place. It's a place where any customer can interact with any company at any time, using any means she chooses. It could be my accessing their website on my BlackBerry, it could be you calling the 800-number, or it could be my mother logging on to the company's Facebook page through her MacBook Pro.

We need to stop thinking about the *how* and start focusing on the *what*. As in, it doesn't matter anymore how a customer connects. What matters is that she has connected. How can we make that customer's experience better, no matter how she connects to us?

Flying home from Toronto today, I got to the airport way early and found that there was an earlier flight. Without a second of hesitation, Porter Airlines changed my flight *and* got me an emergency exit row with extra legroom. I've flown Porter twice before. I'm not frequent with them.

I tweeted from my BlackBerry how cool I thought that was, and they answered me within 10 minutes. It could have been through my Mac, or my Sprint EVO, or one of the free computers at the terminal. *It didn't matter.* What matters is that I'll be flying Porter a lot more often. How I choose to tell the world about my newfound appreciation for Porter is irrelevant.

That's what we have to strive for each and every time. Does it mean hiring someone to strictly handle social media? I don't believe it does, unless you're a multimillion-customer company. I believe it can be distributed amongst the customer service people, the marketing people, and the like. You'll always have people within your company—no matter how small—who love this stuff. Your job is to find them and surprise them by explaining that you believe in this stuff, too, and want them to get more involved.

I guarantee you that right now, in some room, or office, or lab, or college dorm, there's someone working on something big—the next Facebook, the next Twitter, the next *DoodleJump* or *Angry Birds*. (If you have an iPad or iPhone and you haven't

heard of either *DoodleJump* or *Angry Birds*, download them both now. And I'm
sorry for introducing you to that which will destroy your productivity.)

Soon, it's no longer going to be about the platform. It's not going to be about where
I post my status update, or where I talk from, or to whom. It's simply going to be
about *the conversation.*

Your job will become (if it hasn't completely already) simply knowing where the
conversations are happening, monitoring them, and reacting/injecting/conversing
as they do.

And more importantly, your job will be about creating spectacular customer service
so that as you monitor these conversations, they become better and better. That's
truly the goal.

What's that age-old quote?

"Seems that there's never time to do it right the first time, but always time to do it
again?"

Taking that point into consideration, here are your options for today, sir:

> Option 1: Use social media to react to problems when they occur,
> which will be quite frequently because you don't bother going to the
> root of the issue—poor customer service.

> Option 2: Use social media to investigate how your customer service is
> working, improve that which needs improvement, grow that which is
> already great, and then use social media to react to *the much smaller
> number of problems that occur.*

It's up to you, but I think you know the right option.

While the term *social media* is just a buzzword, there's no denying that our country—heck, our world—is undergoing a radical shift in the way information is
received, processed, and shared. I don't think anyone would argue that.

The thing to remember, though, is that it's here to stay. Once exposed, things can
never go back to the way they were. And they never will.

And here's a real mind-bender for you: This is just the very tip of the iceberg. We're
not even at the first 1/10 of 1% of what we're going to see in the future. You think
it's amazing now that Grandma can see photos of her grandchildren in real time
from thousands of miles away when she logs on to her computer? What about in a
few years, when she's able to, right from the store, size her grandkid, just by pressing
a button on her watch? The kid's size and measurements will come right back to
her, and she will be able to buy the right size, right there.

As you're enjoying your amazing dessert, perhaps your tastes—what you're tasting,
such as the vanilla and cinnamon—are being read in real time and being stored in

your "what I like to eat for dessert" notes, which the next person to invite you to dinner can access.

We're not even close to having the ability to begin to imagine what's out there.

And while that's in the future, take this to heart: At one point, the ability to talk to anyone via a device you held up to your ear was in the future. The ability to see inside a live human body didn't exist at one point. Neither did the ability to board a thin metal tube and fly somewhere.

So what does that mean for you?

Well, you can ignore it. That occasionally works out well. Like, for the dinosaurs. Going about their daily lives worked out well for them. Oh, wait....

Or, you can embrace it and get excited about it.

Heck, even if you don't embrace it, at least you can take a mild interest in it.

That's really all I'm asking. Take a mild interest in it. Do a few things a little differently than before. A couple of new ideas here, a few different ways of communicating there.... Before you know it, you're doing this stuff and, more importantly, reaping the rewards.

So, let's review how to do it.

Be "*That* Guy"

In the introduction, we learned that the old rules, the "we'll get to it when we want to get to it" rules, had flown out the door with the teletype and the fax. We've learned that it has quickly turned into "we must listen and react, but even before that, we need to engage the customer to make sure that when problems do occur, we've got the customers, stories, and goodwill on our side to fix them."

The goal as we learned it was to be "that guy." You want to be the guy people listen to and the one people want to hear from. You want to be the one who isn't going to waste anyone's time with BS, but rather who will get to the point and will find the problem, fix it, and get back to the business of making the customer happy. You want to be the one who will figure out the problem before it becomes a megaproblem.

We learned to be "that guy."

The thing about "that guy" that I love the most is that anyone can do it and yet virtually no one does.

As we discussed, when most people *don't* do something simple that can greatly benefit their brand, when you do it, no matter how basic it is, you look like a hero.

I work with a running coach who swears that he doubles his monthly number of "likes" on Facebook simply by asking people when they join the page what their race schedule is.

He makes a note of it and then the day before the race wishes them luck and asks them to post their results on the page as soon as they get them.

When they do, he comments; congratulates them again; and usually gets the comment party started, which results in tons of other congratulations from people all across the land who also "like" his page.

This forms friendships, this forms bonds, and this gets people talking.

You know who's at the center of it all?

Our friend, the coach.

When people outside our coach's world congratulate the runners and say "hey, I should take up running," who do you think gets the call?

Our friend, the coach.

The coach is "that guy." It takes him perhaps 20 minutes *a week*. Results? More clients than he knows what to do with.

Be "that guy." It'll change everything you know about your brand, in a super-good way.

Saddling Up

In Chapter 1, "Putting Together a Social Media Team," we learned about assembling the right armies for the right battles.

It's not all about the tech team. I'd go so far as to say that the tech team is the last group you want to call if the issue at hand isn't entirely tech-related.

You want to start with the customer service group. Chances are, they know the problems the customers have long before anyone else does. Why? They know because they're on the front lines. Back in the days of Sparta, these people were called *runners*. They ran up to the approaching armies (while trying not to be killed) and ran back to the home army to tell them what was about to go down. Runners were invaluable in helping many an army make strategic decisions.

As such, your runners are the people with their ears closest to the ground, listening to the wind. In this case, it's your customer service people. They're the ones on the front lines listening to the complaints the second they come in, when they're still small complaints. They're scanning the message boards, the blogs, Twitter, and Facebook to see what's up when they're still small waves, long before they're super-sized tsunamis.

Remember your customer service people, and treat them well. They're the ones who are going to save your weekends and your sanity by jumping on top of small Tuesday afternoon problems before they become cancel-the-vacation-and-call-in-all-the-troops nightmares.

But you do need more than just customer service. You need marketing, you need upper-management buy-in, and you need the ones in charge to give you the sign-off on what you're doing. But to do that, you need to show them why social media is important and what it can do for your company.

And as we discussed, the best way to do that at all is simply by referencing the almighty dollar.

Thou shalt remember the rule: When it comes to upper-management, revenue trumps cool every time.

It doesn't matter how cool the toy is or how cool it is when everyone retweets your latest post. If what you're doing isn't driving revenue, sales, and the like, upper-management won't see the value in it. If upper-management doesn't see the value, they won't get on board. And we all know what happens when upper-management doesn't get on board: You don't have a social media plan because it has been killed before it has even been let out of the office.

You also want to make friends with the guy in accounting who has a Facebook page, as he can add tremendous value not seen in other departments. And, of course, don't forget the marketing folks. Put them together, and you'll have a kick-ass team.

On the flip side, Chapter 1 also introduced you to the customers. The super-complainer, the one-time complainer, the he-has-never-complained-before complainer—all those fun folks. Remember them. Understand where they come from and how they can affect your business. Remember that, although you should never ignore any customer, some customers have more valid complaints than others and some are worth paying more attention to than others.

Also, try to get inside the complainer's head. What really pissed her off so badly? Was it one event or a series of smaller events? Remember that the more you learn from your complainers, the better you can prevent these problems from happening again.

Social media allows us to listen like never before. In some cases, you can become a student of history and actually watch the event unfold—from the first time the customer complained until the problem is resolved. When you have those opportunities, take full advantage of them. They'll help you improve your processes for the next time and hopefully prevent a repeat-complainer from being born.

Recovering from Social Media Face-plants

Chapter 2, "Examples of When It Doesn't Work (and What Happens)" introduced us to some problems, some famous face-plants, as it were, and showed us the basics of how to avoid what the other guys did.

Had Motrin simply been listening to its audience when the ill-fated baby sling commercial broke, it could have immediately gauged reaction and taken appropriate steps. Instead, it didn't do anything for close to an entire day, and the company paid a huge price for it.

We learned that, by watching and listening, even something as simple as the act of creating a Google News Alert can save you hours, days, or months of frustration later. In fact, it can also save your business.

You need to listen. Want to broadcast? Buy radio time. In this new world we're in, customer service starts first by listening. But by now, you know that, right?

Learn your LUPR rules—listen, understand, plan, and respond. Don't post in a blazing fit of "I'm so sorry!" or, even worse, "I'm so mad!" You'll only lose.

Sit down, figure out what happened, and work on crafting a response that fixes the problem first. When your customers are pissed off, they want an apology, but even more so, they want the situation made right. All the apologies in the world won't do anything for a man who is bumped from his flight and can't get home in time for his daughter's birthday dinner.

Keep one other fact in mind, as well: when problems do happen, they tend to prevent people from doing something, such as catching a flight, getting into a hotel room, using the piece of software they wanted, and so on. That means that once we've encountered a problem, we end up with free time—free time that we might've at one time used to compose a strongly worded letter. Now, that free time is spent broadcasting. The customer *broadcasts* his problems on Twitter, where other people *broadcast* their empathy. If the problem was bad enough, the media might pick it up (think United Breaks Guitars—see "United Breaks Guitars" http://www.youtube.com/watch?v=5YGc4zOqozo)]and *broadcast* it to the world.

What's that old-world phrase? "An idle mind is the devil's workshop"? It could be updated to, "Someone with time to kill could potentially take down your company."

Imagine if you got to the dry cleaners and your suit wasn't ready yet. Right now, it's easy to tweet, "Stupid dry cleaners. How hard is it to have my suit done when you say you will?" But, as more and more people start using GPS-enabled phones for applications such as Foursquare and Gowalla and they integrate with Twitter and Facebook, it becomes a different world:

"Stupid dry cleaners. How hard is it to have my suit done when you say you will?" *—at Joe's Dry Cleaners on 54th and 8th Avenue*

Oops. That would suck.

 Note

Want to learn more about marketing to Foursquare, Gowalla, Yelp, and other social location sharing app users? See *Simon Salt's Social Location Sharing: Outshining Your Competitors on Foursquare, Gowalla, Yelp, and Other Location Sharing Sites*, published by Que.

Let's look at what social media really is. Social media is customer service, pure and simple. And as we discussed, it starts at the granular level—employees and management. It's a way of thinking first and a marketing plan second.

Paying It Forward Pays Off at Crisis Time

If you read Chapter 3, "Before the Explosion: Winning Your Customer," you probably got chills and said at one time or another, "Yeah, I've been there." In that chapter, we discussed crisis management and how social media has catapulted "we have three days before the media picks up on this" to "we just saw our boss being arrested on TMZ," or worse. What do you do?

Remember: everyone is a photojournalist. As I sit here writing this in an airport, I see some idiot in front of me screaming at the gate agent. If I felt like it, I could videotape it with either of the two phones I carry or with my camera and send the video to YouTube. If I happen to walk up to him and look at the ticket, I can tag the video with his name. Oops.

We need to be smarter.

We need to know what's happening as it happens and be prepared to respond the second it does. This includes making sure we know all about our Google News Alerts and making sure we can respond the second something happens.

There's no excuse nowadays for not having the most up-to-date information on anything you happen to be looking for or talking about.

Funnily, as I typed that sentence, the gate agent just told us we were 30 minutes delayed. I went to flight-stats.com and found out we were actually 1 hour and 30 minutes delayed!

No excuse for not having the latest data. Do your homework, and look it up. Create your social media crisis plan and get buy-in on it long before you ever have to possibly use it.

There's a saying in skydiving: "Mid-air is no time to become a rigger." What that means, essentially, is that if you have a problem that may or may not be fixable right after you open your parachute and you can't fix it with a good shake of the canopy, you jettison it and open your reserve.

The same rule applies in social media crisis situations. You don't want to have to write a plan while the "Ding! Ding! Ding!" of new bad news emails chimes in the background.

Know what you're going to do. Drill it into your head and the head of those who will be involved. Have a contact list and a call sheet.

 Tip

> Make sure you have 100% corporate buy-in on your social media crisis management plan long before anything ever happens, so you're able to immediately implement it without having to wait for any type of approval. Social Media doesn't wait for committee meetings to judge you, your brand, or your business.

Remember the "one voice" rule. Want to have some fun? Call a company the next time you're trying to return a product. Ask some random question that you know isn't in the script the call center follows and listen to the answer. Then call back, get someone else and do the same thing. You'll likely get a completely different answer. That's the fun of not sticking to one voice.

When you have a crisis, there needs to only be one voice. Not several, not a group consensus in public, but one voice. That one voice is going to run the company response, and that's the voice that speaks.

There's a reason the President of the United States has a press secretary, and not 20 people in the White House speaking for him.

You'll want to know your troops. Know who to use for specific battles. The thing about that is to make sure you know that battles can change and, as such, so should troops. Are the same people in the same positions they were in when the original plan was drafted?

A plan is fluid. It's supposed to be able to change. That's why it's a plan. Good plans change when they need to.

So, once you get the right people, go back to the part where we talked about knowing your audience. You know how they get their information, how they *prefer* to get their information, right? Right? You know what their preferred format is, too, right? You should. We talked about this earlier. You want to be able to make sure that they have the words, from you, in the way they prefer to get them. That way, you'll be able to amass your audience and make them work for *you*. You've spent so much time building up banks of good will. This is where you want to cash in some of it.

Reaching out to your audience to tell them about the problem and how you're going to fix it is a good thing. Reaching out to your audience on a random Wednesday just to say hi and offer 10% off because you like making them happy is a much, much better thing. This will turn them into the kind of fans you want when you have a problem.

Remember that when you *do* talk to your audience about your screw-up, that's the time to be precise, not to blame. You don't want to be too apologetic, and you definitely don't want to get angry. Your job is to admit you screwed up and then get back to your job of *fixing the problem*. Keeping your customers updated on your progress will work in your favor.

Working with a visual problem? Use visual aids to fix it. Visual works when you can show progress. Go get a flip cam and show your progress.

Get a person out in front of the audience and have her do a video. Apology videos, when done right, always work better than apology letters. (This offer isn't valid when you're trying to apologize to your girlfriend for forgetting her birthday.)

Don't give up. Remember consistency because that's what sails the ship. That's what you need. Don't play into the haters' hands and don't respond to them in chat rooms, on message boards, or through Twitter.

Try to run your response by legal. (I had to say that.)

Don't lie. You remember that, right?

The crisis will pass, people will find someone else to be angry at, and if you're smart you can use it as a learning experience to help grow your company vision the next time something happens. It's all part of the cycle of life.

Learn It. Know It. Live It.

Next, we hit Chapter 4, "Customer Service Is a Way of Life," which talked about customer service being a way of life, how your brand is perceived by the public, and the fact that your online and offline brand are simply going to merge and form one super-brand that's capable of destroying the universe—and you need to be ready for that.

Okay, your brand won't really destroy the universe, but you'd better be aware that the difference between a personal and private brand will no longer exist. What will exist in its place will simply be your brand. How you choose to grow that brand, online, offline, at 2 in the afternoon or 3 in the morning, will determine how people perceive the brand, the company, you, and anything connected to the brand.

Look at the case studies provided in Chapter 4. Looking at something as simple as Dalch Wellness—started by one woman—shows the power of providing valuable information. If it's information your audience wants, they'll be clamoring to get it, and it's not self-promotion if it's help. If you're helping people by providing stuff they need, they'll never look at is as promotion. Rather, they'll say thank you, share it with friends, and help grow your base.

Lara Dalch asks a simple question a few times a week and promotes engagement. People communicate with her and she responds. I'd rather have 100 people who communicated with me on a regular basis than 10,000 fans who couldn't care less that they were on my page. Full disclosure time: Lara's a friend, but that doesn't take away from the fact that she's doing it right.

Remember the bakery and the cups near Central Park? What can you do that costs a few bucks a week that can generate tremendous results?

Remember that the content you create has the power to make people happy, and when people like what you've created, they want to share it, whether it's a Cadbury commercial for an ostrich or a video on the best way to spend your weekend. Either way, you have the opportunity—no, the privilege—of creating compelling content that will engage your audience, make them want to share, and (most importantly) make them want to buy from you. That's your job.

Remember that social media also lets you turn bad into good. You can find things that could be disasters and reach out much more easily than ever before. Check out Which Wich and what they did when they found a customer who'd broken his jaw biting into one of their sandwiches. They made a new friend and got millions of dollars in free publicity. Their efforts took them just one weekend.

Any of these case studies in Chapter 4 can be easily applied to your company. They all have several key items in common:

- The company realizes there is a need to communicate.

- The company understands there's a way to not only disseminate information, but also to invite conversation and promote two-way dialogue.

- The company attempts, in several ways, to integrate item two (a two-way exchange of information).

- The company increases what works and decreases what doesn't.

When you think about it, that's not too hard.

The deal I made with you in Chapter 4 still stands: Come up with an idea and then send me an email about it (peter@shankman.com). Let me take a look and see if I can't suggest any other ideas that might work. But don't email me with "hey, what social media idea should I implement?" That's boring.

Head 'em Off at the Pass

The small problems and the pain in the ass were both introduced in Chapter 5, "Social Media Damage Control: Stopping Small Problems from Becoming Big Ones." Remember that small problems can hurt you a lot more than large problems can.

The small problem can be your biggest problem if you don't address it quickly. The small complainer 30 years ago didn't have the microphone he has now.

Understand the complainers out there and start categorizing all of them. Make sure you know which kind of complainer you're dealing with before you engage him. You might not even need to engage him that much or for that long. A lot of times, a simple "sorry that happened, we'll hook you up with X" will do the trick.

Sometimes, though, you need more.

Keep track of the customers. Write down what they do and why they complain. Remember: crunching data is the key to good customer response.

If you find customers on Twitter, check them out on Klout (www.klout.com) as well as all the other sources.

Reach out, listen, and react. Apologize, but focus on fixing the problem. That will shut up 99% of all the complainers. Go from there.

Most importantly, turn them into fans. Fans rock. Fans tell other people to become fans. Fans preach your good word.

You want people preaching your good word.

Make the solution worth them preaching:

> "Hey @multicomplainer – Sorry to hear your bread wasn't fresh during your last visit to Joe's – Let us know the next time you want to come in, and we'll buy you and three friends a round of drinks on Joe"

Remember that some complainers want the problem fixed first and the apology second. Understand that when the never-complained-before-customer actually does complain, he doesn't care that you're sorry. Your customer doesn't want to hear, "We understand you're upset." All your customer wants to hear is that you're fixing the problem and that the resolution will occur at X time, at Y place, resulting in Z satisfaction.

You gotta get on that.

Listen. React. Make it right.

How you choose to listen is up to you, but make sure you do it.

In fact, I'd go on record and say that just listening first and reacting second can correct 50% of all problems.

Everyone has a camera with them nowadays. Everyone. So make sure you know how to deal with the multimedia complainer. Can you send her a free camera to document the good stuff you're doing now that you've fixed the problem?

Make her happy, and she'll be your friend for life.

I've said it countless times: It comes down to customer service.

Creating Customers for Life

Chapter 6, "Making Customer Addicts Online: Best Practices that Work!," was fun. It was all about addiction. Turning customers into addicts, as I showed you, it wasn't anywhere near as hard as it might have seemed.

Remember WARS:

> **W**elcome
>
> **A**ppreciated
>
> **R**eturn
>
> **S**hare

You want customers to feel welcome and appreciated, and you want them to return and share.

If I feel welcome in a store, a hotel, an airport, a lounge, a club, a restaurant, anywhere, I'm more than likely to feel appreciated. The two go hand in hand, wouldn't you agree?

If I don't feel welcome when I come in, the whole experience is tainted. Chances are, I won't have any desire to return.

Recently, I made a reservation at Morton's. While making the reservation, they asked if it was for anything special. I told them that I was training for a triathlon and this would be my last meal before I went into hardcore training. Imagine my surprise when I got to my table and saw that the menu contained a message wishing me luck! See Figure 9.1. You know I felt welcome!

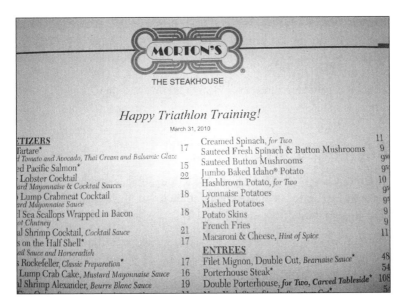

Figure 9.1 *Talk about feeling welcome!*

Keep in mind that I said welcomed, and not stalked. Don't stalk. That's creepy. If you were a customer being welcomed in the way you're welcoming your customer, would you be cool with it?

Make sure you know your audience. Getting an email that's totally off base after I've visited shows me that you don't care.

However, if you're learning about your audience and you know some other things they've posted publicly, there's nothing wrong with a follow-up. I've seen some restaurants watch their Twitter feeds and when they see someone tweet about needing a drink, they invite them in for a drink on the house.

That works! Without customers, you wouldn't be here. You wouldn't be reading this book. You wouldn't be doing much of anything. Customers pay the bills. Without them, you're history. Or to quote *Mad Men*, "They can shut off our lights."

You want to keep your lights on.

Remember that people aren't numbers, customers aren't automated response devices, and we all like to be thought of as human beings.

Can you give your employees (or yourself) one hour a week where they can just follow up with customers to say hi? Not pitching, not selling, not filling a sales cycle, but just saying hi?

Sharing is caring. Just saying, "We're sending this discount to you for you to share with your friends" makes your customer feel like a hero.

We all like feeling like heroes.

Don't forget the "Tweet This!" or "Share This on Facebook!" button on your website. Why not let your customers spread the love?

Addicts love to get something extra. Give them that and they'll come back for more, every time.

Thinking Like a Drug Dealer

Still with me? Chapter 7, "Keeping the Addiction Going," taught us all the little tips and tricks we can do to get and keep our audience's addiction going strong— including how to think like a drug dealer! That was fun to write!

You've got to remember that people, thanks to social media, have become a little bit fickle. Why do you think frequent flier programs are so successful? Airlines give you something for free if you're loyal.

The irony there is that they're giving you things for free now that used to be free but now aren't anymore, such as no baggage fees—but that's neither here nor there.

You've got to remember to make your customers loyal. Anything you put out has to be something people will want again and again. Why? Because if they see it once and don't like it, they won't bother coming back. Ever.

The good quality rule: If the quality sucks, no one is gonna come back.

Speak only when you have something to say. Talk when you have something worth talking about. Too many emails spoil the newsletter broth. You get the idea.

How often do you see an email that makes you buy what they're selling on the spot? Not that often. Usually, the email that makes you buy comes not just by one email, but by a host of emails and reach-outs that, over time, make you aware that the product is a good one. Then, when they hit you with the right scenario at the right time, you buy.

That's what you're looking for when you're trying to keep the addiction going.

Be more compelling than anyone else and know your audience better than anyone else. Otherwise, it won't matter how compelling you are because they won't be your audience anymore.

I always find it funny when people come up to me at conferences and can't understand why no one engages them on their Facebook pages or Twitter streams. "It's like they don't care!"

Well, once I take a look at their pages and streams and realize that they've never offered anything of value via those outlets, it's an easy fix.

Remember this again and again and again: It is not a RIGHT to be able to talk to your audience, or to even have an audience at all. It is a PRIVILEGE. Without fulfilling your responsibility of creating compelling, interesting content, there's absolutely no reason for any audience member to continue following you or to bother trying to engage your brand.

Don't forget that there's a giant world out there! Don't just waste time repeating nothing but information about your products. You've got a world of information from which you can pull: news, information, famous birthdays, you name it! What can you do to pull that information into your reach-outs, emails, and the like?

I love to see (and usually act on) emails that have some tie-in to what's going on in the world. Remember SeamlessWeb? (It's pouring, order soup!) They know how to reach an audience that really needs it right when they really need it.

The Right Tool for the Job

Chapter 8, "Monitoring Your Successes and Failures," was all about the tools—how to use them and how to make sure they work for you. I'm not going to repeat any of that here. You can reread it. The fact is, you have a good range of mostly free tools to use to monitor, control, and grow your social media network. Use as many as you'd like. They're all there, all for the taking. Use whichever ones work for you.

A Few Final Words

Okay...so you've only got a few pages left of the book. You're still awake, and still reading it. You haven't lapsed into a coma, or worse, started falling into uncontrollable seizures. That's a good thing.

If I jumped right out of the book pages right now and asked you what you thought the central themes of it were, what would you say?

- Customer service, obviously.

- Social media and how to use it, sure.

- Generating happy customers who can help create your growth. Definitely.

But what about two more?

What about being different and having fun? I don't think we take those two thoughts into account when we work. We don't like to be different for some reason, and we sure as heck don't consider work "fun."

The funny thing is, I do! I've *always* loved to be different, and I've always loved to have fun. I never thought I wasn't allowed to do either at work, and in the few jobs I had where I worked for someone else, I was fortunate to be able to have fun and be myself, as well.

So perhaps that's the real take-away here. If you're having a good time, then it's probably easier to continue what you're doing. Can you keep having a good time and making what you're doing work better for your company, your business, and your brand? Can you incorporate a little more of your personal brand into your business and approach your customers a little more as "friends" and a little less as "User2714?"

Can you make it so that people actually enjoy their time at your establishment, want to come back, and tell their friends? If people have a great time, they're more likely to share that great time and consider your business a friend. You want to be considered a friend. You don't want to be considered "just another way for someone to get what she needs."

What fun is that?

I've said before that the goal of social media is to generate revenue. That's correct. I stand by that. But I also think it's to have fun and to enjoy ourselves. I think that social media allows for unprecedented access to our customers, to our fans, and even to our detractors. If we can use it to the best of our ability to generate fans and friends, the money will come. I promise it will. It always does.

I hope I've given you some new ways of thinking, some good ideas, and some fun projects you can implement right now to start that process.

Did I miss anything? You know how to find me:

> peter@shankman.com
>
> http://shankman.com
>
> http://facebook.com/petershankman
>
> http://twitter.com/petershankman
>
> http://foursquare.com/user/petershankman
>
> http://plancast.com/shankman will tell you when I'm in your city speaking. Email me and let's grab a coffee.
>
> Finally, http://shankman.com/calendar tells you what city I'm in when. Send me an email. Chances are we can meet up.

I'd love for you to drop me a note and tell me what you thought. How can I improve for the next printing?

Finally, remember this: The goal of the journey isn't the destination. The goal of the journey is the journey itself. Remember to enjoy it. Learn from it. Each thing you do, each idea you implement, each action you take—whether in social media, the real world, your business, or your personal life—affects other decisions you make and helps keep you on course for the next fun event. And that, well, that's kind of cool.

Enjoy the ride, have fun, and be safe. Blue skies!

Photo courtesy of Becky Johns, www.becky-johns.com

Index

B

C

D

E

Q–R

S

QUE®
Biz-Tech Series

Straightforward Strategies and Tactics for Business Today

The **Que Biz-Tech series** is designed for the legions of executives and marketers out there trying to come to grips with emerging technologies that can make or break their business. These books help the reader know what's important, what isn't, and provide deep inside know-how for entering the brave new world of business technology, covering topics such as mobile marketing, microblogging, and iPhone and iPad app marketing.

- Straightforward strategies and tactics for companies who are either using or will be using a new technology/product or way of thinking/ doing business

- Written by well-known industry experts in their respective fields— and designed to be an open platform for the author to teach a topic in the way he or she believes the audience will learn best

- Covers new technologies that companies must embrace to remain competitive in the marketplace and shows them how to maximize those technologies for profit

- Written with the marketing and business user in mind—these books meld solid technical know-how with corporate-savvy advice for improving the bottom line

   Visit **quepublishing.com/biztech** to learn more about the **Que Biz-Tech series**

Peter Shankman

Peter's a buzzsaw of ideas. The big risk is that your head will explode before you implement this all.
—Chris Brogan, President Human Business Works and publisher

Customer
New Rules for a Social Media World

Service

FREE Online Edition

Your purchase of *Customer Service: New Rules for a Social Media World* includes access to a free online edition for 45 days through the Safari Books Online subscription service. Nearly every Que book is available online through Safari Books Online, along with more than 5,000 other technical books and videos from publishers such as Addison-Wesley Professional, Cisco Press, Exam Cram, IBM Press, O'Reilly, Prentice Hall, and Sams.

SAFARI BOOKS ONLINE allows you to search for a specific answer, cut and paste code, download chapters, and stay current with emerging technologies.

Activate your FREE Online Edition at
www.informit.com/safarifree

> **STEP 1:** Enter the coupon code: MTGOHAA.

> **STEP 2:** New Safari users, complete the brief registration form.
> Safari subscribers, just log in.

If you have difficulty registering on Safari or accessing the online edition, please e-mail customer-service@safaribooksonline.com

Safari
Books Online

Addison Wesley   AdobePress   ALPHA   Cisco Press   FT Press   IBM Press   lynda.com   Microsoft Press   New Riders

O'REILLY   Peachpit Press   PRENTICE HALL   que   Redbooks   SAMS   SAS Publishing   Sun   WILEY